I KNOW THE HUMAN MIND

Unlock the Mysteries Within

RAMESH SINGH PAL

BlueRose ONE.com
Stories Matter
NewDelhi • London

BLUEROSE PUBLISHERS
India | U.K.

BlueRose ONE
Stories Matter
NewDelhi • London

For permissions requests or inquiries regarding this publication,
please contact:

BLUEROSE PUBLISHERS
www.BlueRoseONE.com
info@bluerosepublishers.com
+91 8882 898 898
+4407342408967

ISBN: 978-93-7018-289-9

Cover Design: Shubham Verma
Typesetting: Sagar

First Edition: May 2025

Preface

Whether mind should be placed among the cause of anxiety, pain or suffering or among the cause of happiness, calmness and bliss may perhaps be regarded as a doubtful question. To recognize the human mind is indeed the first reason for seeking the transcendental truth. Scriptures *Vedanta, Upanishad, Bhagavad Gita* proclaim that one can use mind as a tool for divinity.

Human mind is vast, complex and indefinable and cannot be cast into the mould of a narrow definition. Mind is the fountain-head of inspiration to poets and philosophers in every age. Mind is the source of creativity for mathematicians, astronomers and physicists. It requires a sensitive soul and a spirit of adventure to know the secrets of human mind.

This book "*I Know the Human Mind*" doesn't mean to entertain or preach readers, but to make them 'think' to develop a deeper understanding of their inner subtle world and the outer gross world around them. The book doesn't reveal anything 'new' concepts of mind, but rather sheds light on the elusive truths you have encountered yet couldn't express it in words.

The human mind is a complex and mysterious entity, capable of incredible feats of creativity, innovation and progress. Yet, it can also be a source of suffering, anxiety and self-doubt. In a comprehensive 15-chapter book including conclusion, the intricacies of the mind are explored, offering readers a valuable asset to understand and master their own minds.

Chapter 1-3 Understanding the Mind

The book begins by delving into the basics of the brain, mind and consciousness. The author explores the basic understanding of the functions of the brain and how it differs from mind and consciousness. The author discuss the different states of mind-- waking, sleeping and deep sleep; and how consciousness witness all the states of mind. The chapters also deal with how the different states of mind impact your thoughts, emotions and actions.

Chapter 4-6 Working of Mind

The next chapters focus on the inner and outer factors that have an impact on the working patterns of mind. The author throws light on the individual mind and the collective mind. The multiplicity of world exists owing to the different types of mind. The author delves deeper into the working style of mind and how persons react differently in the same situation.

Chapters 7-9 Psychology of Mind

The chapter deals with how you think, feel and behave in a tough situation. In the following chapters, the author explores psychology of mind including the evolution of mind. He tries to prove that it has the power to completely alter all your previous perceptions and method of thinking. It helps you learn how you react and act certain ways and how your mind work. Mind has three parts thoughts, emotions and behavior. One can improve his thoughts, feelings and actions by practicing and learning new things.

Chapter 10-12 Power of Mind

Mind is the cause of all fear and anxiety. And, interestingly it has the power to overcome fear, anxiety and doubt. The author proposes pragmatic approach to turn you optimistic by overcoming daily life obstacles just by using the power of your mind. A relaxed, peaceful and stable mind lives a meaningful life compared to a disturbed and chaotic mind.

Chapter 13-15 Tools for Divinity & Conclusion

The mind is a stranger to the sleepy man, a source of confusion and chaos. But to the wise, it's a loyal companion that remains with him in odd and even situations. A relaxed, peaceful and stable mind lives a meaningful life compared to a disturbed and chaotic mind. When mind becomes pure and desire-less, the practitioner undergoes divine and blissful experiences. These experiences open the doors of wisdom and unravel various mysteries of life.

By reading and understanding this book, you will identify thought-patterns, emotions, and feelings to change everything in your favor. By applying the principles outlined in this book, readers can transform their moving minds into tools of learning and wisdom, leading to individual growth, cordial relationship and a more fulfilling and appealing life.

Finally, it is hoped that this book will be quite useful to the research scholars, school students and seekers of Truth. Suggestions for further improvement of the book are welcome.

Ramesh Pal.

(Ramesh Singh Pal)

Contents

Chapter 1
Introduction 1

Chapter 2
Brain vs. Mind 4

Chapter 3
Mind vs. Consciousness 21

Chapter 4
How Mind Works? 36

Chapter 5
Individual Mind vs. Collective Mind 53

Chapter 6
Types of Mind 69

Chapter 7
No-Mind State 87

Chapter 8
Psychology of Mind 103

Chapter 9
Evolution of Mind 120

Chapter 10
Balancing the Mind 134

Chapter 11
Power of Human Mind 150

Chapter 12
Ultimate Use of Mind....165

Chapter 13
Mind: Tool for Divinity....177

Chapter 14
Beyond Mind....189

Chapter 15
Conclusions....197

Chapter 1

Introduction

Watching ever-flowing gurgling Ganga or hearing soul-stirring song of forest bird or smelling aromatic fragrance of beautiful rose, mind absorbs the whole experience. It leaves an indelible impression on your consciousness. Science says all are the impressions of human mind. The whole experience depends on the intensity of feeling through five cognitive senses.

Life is flooded with incidents--good or bad, pleasant or unpleasant, joyful or piercing. Call it a blessing or curse of nature; mind is witness of all. Whether you recall happiest days or horrible dark nights; it's up to you how you consider life. It's the nature of human mind to remember painful moments of life but forget pleasing hours of days gone by.

Human mind is a process of thinking. Mind is so flexible that it can rotate in 360 degree. If you want to be successful in life, then nothing is more powerful than mind. A poet uses his pensive mind to write poem; mathematician logical mind to solve geometric puzzle and politician uses his calculative mind to assure win in elections. Mind is utilitarian.

The world is ever-changing and has no essence; it is merely reflection of human minds. An enlightened yogi sees divinity everywhere; but to a pickpocket, the world is nothing but pockets.

For a child, the world is dawn, symbolizing hope, innocence and wonder. While the same world is dusk for an old man representing old memories and faded past.

Philosophers proclaim that as many minds, as many the worlds. Mind sees the world in a different way and everything you see is a perspective, not the truth. Ordinary mind clings to whatever it finds fascinating. Reality has nothing to do with flickering, but it remains same whatever your state of mind may be.

Mind divides the unified existence. What you see through mind is always illusory. Illusionary world means where you can't differentiate between what is real and what is unreal. Duality is not in nature, it is in ignorant mind. Mind is accustomed to unreal world. You can't transcend the world where you live, but can use it as a bridge to reach new dimension of awareness.

'Illusionary' word doesn't indicate that the world that you perceive in day-to-day life doesn't exist. Instead, illusion is in your perception because you see the world through the conditioned mind. You create an unreal world because of your projections. When you see the world without judgment of good or bad, only then you see the world as it is.

Whatsoever you perceive through five senses in the world is the reflection of minds. If it looks like full of promises, it means it is your reflection. If it looks like fear and uncertainty, again it is your reflection. As you see many suns in pots of water, so the different mind see the same world differently. Human mind is complex, indescribable and ever-changing like the river.

Mind is the core of your imagination and creativity. The untrained and unkempt mind needs to be disciplined. To sustain life, mind is pre-requisite. To think of the past or plan of the future mind helps you in all possible way. It has to move in the right direction to yield the output of your efforts. But keep in mind that you are not the mind.

Fluctuating Mind

The nature of human mind is to fluctuate. It takes the form of countless thoughts moment to moment. Happiness and depression are just two states of mind. Happiness and worry, success and failure, love and hate are polarities of life. Everything looks pleasant, while you feel happy. Life becomes irksome, when you are depressed.

Human mind is a bridge between the beast and the divine. You have the experience of beast because you are in the cycle of birth and death. But divine is not in your domain, it's a distant dream. A pure mind with no desires and dreams is divine. A mind filled with anger, hatred, and jealousy is beast. Upanishad says mind is the cause of bondage or freedom. Only the proper understanding of the mind enables you to purify, elevate and enlighten the mind to attain freedom from doubts, sorrow, fear and worries.

मन एव मनुष्याणां कारणं बन्धमोक्षयोः।
बन्धाय विषयासक्तं मुक्त्यैनिर्विषयंस्मृतम्॥ (अमृतबिन्दुपनिषद्, 6/34)

Whatever happens in mind is ephemeral. You are bound by ignorance, attachment and ego. Pay attention to your thoughts, emotions and feelings without judgment. They appear and disappear, but there is something in you which remain changeless. This helps calm your fickle mind and connect with your divine 'Self'.

---OM---

Chapter 2

Brain vs. Mind

Life is like a rollercoaster. Ups and downs are games of life. There are jubilant moments of happiness and there are also moments of failure and rejection. The human tendency is to blame not using his brain in the nick of time to grab opportunity. But the mind blames the destiny. Only an active brain and steady mind can help you to navigate your ship in every storm. The key lies in how and where this power of mind is channelized.

Knowing needs an accepting mind. Feel in your mind what the brain stores information of knowing. Every information or data has to go deep into mind, underneath and hidden. In many cases, many human don't feel they need to learn anything because they presume they already know the whole thing. It happens because mind encounters the temptation of the world.

Brain is potent yet mysterious tool of knowing; and more intricate is the mind. If brain is a computer; then mind is its processor. If you are science student or scholar, you can understand by this metaphor. Brain and mind are concentric circles with the same center i.e. consciousness. Mind is a circle with larger radius because it remains active day and night.

Brain relaxes when you sleep or take a rest. It helps in rejuvenating and refreshing 100 billion neuron cells. As mind is subtle and non-material; it doesn't need any rest. Some part of mind remains active even during deep sleep. That's why brain knows nothing what happened to you during hours of deep sleep, but mind feels it and create mystic experiences.

If you are art student or scholar, you can compare brain and mind by simple figure of speech. Brain is a verb that shows action like whether you are listening, smelling, touching or seeing. Whenever you see something, or taste something delicious; it's the brain which is working gathering information through senses. Mind symbolizes adjective (a feeling in your mind).

Sometimes, brain is unable to digest the content of the topic which you read or hear from your master. When this happens, frustration and anger accrue in your mind. Understanding and emotions are two separate entities that interact and influence each other. Knowing is mental cognitions, whereas emotions are intense feelings related to your mind.

Calculating Brain

Brain is calculating that weighs pros and cons of your every act, planning or working for a dream project. Brain instructs: "change your mind or opinion or decision if it doubts or smell any fishy. But once you make up your mind, never look back. Mind has the potential to think independently and freely that can ensure to bring reward in your kit.

Brain is the simplest unit of mind that collects data and warns you if see any impending danger. That danger can be real or unreal; it's the mind that infers this input (of brain) and provides you the deeper meaning of the observable fact. Just reacting on the input of sensory organs can land you in difficult situation. Your mind is your trusty companion.

Brain is a vital organ and is the hub of human activity. It is the seat of sensory faculties and coordinates and stimulates all the sense organs. It acts as an interface between various organs of the body. It controls nerve signals to various parts of the body. The two characteristic of brain are logic and calculation and is known as prefrontal cortex in medical science.

Life has become so multifaceted that you need brain all over the place to ease your trouble. The calculating brain is dictating your whole affairs and accordingly you don't see the world as it is. There is no place for feelings and emotions in the organ of the mind. Whenever you meet a person first-time, brain weighs all the pros and cons of cultivating it into new relationship.

Shrimad *Bhagavat Gita* says-

व्यवसायात्मिका बुद्धिरेकेह कुरुनन्दन।
बहुशाखा ह्यनन्ताश्च बुद्धयोऽव्यवसायिनाम्।।2.41।।

The knowledge in the form of determination is just one; but the knowledge (thoughts) of those who do not have determination, has many branches and has no end.

Be it office or home, you are so brain-driven, that feelings have almost dry-up. You start finding the fault in others without looking at your heart. The brain is a world consisting of countless possibilities, but mind has the creative power in making the intangible tangible. To get on a transformative journey within, you need the balance of both (mind and brain).

Bee can't make honey alone. Just as the bee needs the flower to create the honey, human need both brain and mind in creating something beautiful and meaningful. To understand the logical riddle of science, you need to engage your brain; and to understand emotions and complexities of human relationships, one can harness the power of mind.

Any action is a result of interaction between brain and mind. Brain is a data of thoughts. Positive or negative thoughts both are subtle forms of energy that have direct impact on the level of awareness. Knowledge comes from data. Mind knows what to accept and what to discard from the accumulated data.

Imagination is the creation of mind. But no imagination is possible without 'words'. Brain helps in shaping your thoughts thus enabling you to construct and express your imagination. Both works together to develop creativity, drive away negative energy and allow increased flow of positive energy from higher dimension of awareness.

Your brain is a fountain-head of all thoughts. It's the mind which divides thoughts into good or bad; positive or negative; creative or destructive. Thinking never happens through brain. Mind moves through associations as mind is the thinker. Mind is the subject in relation to the brain. It is the mind which makes the brain purposeful.

Carl Gustav Jung said: "The brain is an organ of thought, but the mind is the thinker."

Brain is the structural/morphological part of human body and mind is the functional output of morphological brain

How Mind Can Become Your Best Friend?

Stephen Hawking wrote somewhere: "We are just an advanced breed of monkeys on a minor planet of a very average star. But we can understand the Universe. That makes us something very special." If mind leaks energy through negative emotion and self-indulgence, then it is your worst enemy. Define and recognize where you feel conflicted or uncertain.

Don't forget that your mind is the greatest healing force. One can use his imagination and always look for the upward shift. The mind is everything. If the mind loses its liberty, you lose yours. If the mind is free, you are free. Learn to change your perceptions of people by cultivating a positive relationship. Only then your mind can become your best friend.

- **Turn your attention inside:** Turn your attention inside to recognize your thoughts and become aware of your inner world. Ask your inner guide to expand your strength.
- **Restrict your inner space:** No one is perfect in this world. Accept your imperfections silently without allowing anyone to share your inner space.
- **Look before you leap:** Think carefully in your brain and mind both before planning anything or taking any action. A stitch in time saves nine.
- **Be strong and wise:** In a challenging situation, be courageous and bold enough to pull out, rather than be defeated and rejected by unpleasant and hard situations.
- **Be optimistic:** See an opportunity in every calamity and don't be hopeless even when the whole world is against you.
- **Cultivate Hobby:** When you do something closer to your heart, your mind feels elated and undivided. It gives you strength and zeal to move on like a winner.
- **Don't procrastinate anything:** It is worthwhile to execute your work or duty at the right and proper time. Remember, the early bird catches the worm.
- **Positive outlook:** There are many angles to look the same thing. The knife can injure your hand but knife in the hands of surgeon can save the life of a patient.
- **Be supportive:** Every person has their own angle on charity. Whenever get an opportunity, be ready to help the poor and needy.

- **Be silent:** Don't speak if there is no need. If speech is silver than silence is gold as the saying goes. Silence is the highest and most effective language.

The mind is deeper than ocean. It has many jewels hidden within it. The purpose of following these steps is to discover your pure and non-demanding mind. These steps of turning your mind friend are sleek and effective. It's not ordinary mind but mind of wisdom and has a therapeutic effect on your physical, emotional and spiritual well-being.

How powerful is Mind?

What neuron is to brain; conditioning is to mind. Mind is free to move anywhere and at any time. There is no limitation. No doubt, mind is fast-moving, but it can be tamed to make it disciplined and organized. Then, it can be a source of unlimited joy. Before you make your mind the best friend, you have to learn how brain and mind works.

Brain works in day time when there is liveliness around you; and when there is something for senses to stimulate. When there is no sensory input, brain turns to sleeping mode. Contrary to this, when world stops, the mind goes on working. Mind starts imagining, dreaming and recollecting past memories. Mind remains awake even when neural activity slows down.

Mind like human life itself begins in darkness (in the womb of mother). You need to admit this. Brain thinks only in terms of light when everything is visible, perceivable and acceptable to your intelligence. A part of your total consciousness is in your brain, and remaining in your mind. When you are alone, bereft of any thoughts or dreams, you become only consciousness.

Brain is world of thoughts. Thought means a pattern of understandable 'words' mutually agreed upon by all. This gives birth to a language. A child takes years to understand language.

Mind is space of emotion and feelings. A child whose brain is yet to develop still expresses his/her feelings and emotions. Every child is born with a mind and seed of brain.

Brain requires language to express your feelings and emotions. Brain knows and mind knows that you know. Brain receives the information from outer world through five cognitive senses and mind reacts to it. Brain and mind are eccentric circles with a common centre. That centre is consciousness. Consciousness is underlying truth behind the working of your mind and brain.

Brain is the need of life. It is the fundamental and integral part of human existence. Animals, birds and other creatures are also gifted with innate brain. Human is no exception. Mind is the process of dreaming and desiring. Animals and birds live in the present moment; there is no past or future in their life. Man is loaded with both (brain and mind).

Brain and mind are often used interchangeably. Instead, they are two contrasting forces. Brain is gross; while mind is subtle. Brain is part of your physical existence; but mind is related to your mental body and is closer to your innermost core (Self). Mind is a bigger picture that controls your intelligence (brain) to see the light of appeared world clearly.

Suppose you crack a competitive examination in a first attempt. Your brain acknowledges this achievement by reading the text of the call letter. At the same time, your dreaming mind starts envisioning a bigger picture. You begin dreaming of owning a beautiful palatial home and a charming wife. What accounted for this two varying reactions? The answer is clear.

A brain shows the real fact that it knows. Brain only processes the facts, but mind is dreamer that carries you towards a future. The brain calculates, but the mind feels; the brain knows, but the mind understands. When the erratic mind takes on a fact, you become confused. Mind is indeed hard to move in a simple linear path.

Inner World & Outer World

You live in two worlds at the same time. One is outer world of objects and other is inner world of feelings and dreaming. You feel joyous when mind is not loaded with worry, misery and dreams. You feel as if you are floating or levitating. You don't feel any danger from the outer world. Your mind is not filled with any thoughts.

Brain is not a dreamer; you can analyze, plan and manage it to make your outer world suitable. Brain perceives the world mechanically with no touch of emotions and feelings. But when the same information of brain passes through the lens of mind, everything becomes distorted (mind is not balanced). Mind is dreaming process that takes you beyond the confines

Brain is totally different from the mind. Brain is related to your outer world, while mind is knower of your inner world. It's the brain that process sensory information, recognizes patterns, and understands the physical world. Mind is a contracted form of consciousness. Since consciousness is the trait of 'Self' (*atma*), so mind is nearer to your true nature.

It's the mind that lives in fantasies; see imagines possibilities, and dream of imaginary world. While the brain sees the present, the mind sees the future. As a complete human being, you need to trust the both. Scientists and doctors need to rely on their brain while performing experiments in laboratory or conducting operations in hospital.

Mind: Abode of Dreams

The whole world is divine dream. There is no essence in this appeared or manifested world. As mind is part of subtle world, so it begins to weave and create dreams in your leisure time. You remain unaware of your inner dreaming because brain becomes dysfunctional. Dream is not unreal, but included part of your reality. Life is nothing but experiences; and your consciousness also go through experiences in dreaming state.

Dreaming is an act of the mind, not the intellect (brain). Mind is part of subtle world which is much bigger than your outer world. It can accommodate your past and future too. Future is only projection of the dreaming mind into reality of that which already exists. Dream is the seed of every reality. Reality exists in mind in the form of seed. The brain then takes over, nurturing and watering those seeds through pragmatic approach.

The mind is the realm of dreams, where the laws of science are inapplicable, and what brain thinks 'impossible' becomes 'possible'. It's where creativity knows no boundary, and innovation is born. The brain may try to rationalize, but the mind knows no limits. So, when we dream, it's not the brain that's at work, but the mind, weaving a space full of possibilities, hopes, and desires. The brain may see the world in simple black and white, but the mind sees it in rainbow colors, full of promise and potential.

Stephen King writes: "The dreamer's mind is a closed system, where ideas go to die." A closed mind is unwilling to consider new ideas, new thoughts and new visions. Learn to think independently and freely to feel calm and secure. An open mind is hope of endless possibilities. Consequently, you will gain a deeper understanding of life's meaning and value.

Brain: Process only Surface Reality

Indeed your brain is a bit more complex than you seem to realize. How? Just consider that the statement "reality is what your brain can perceive" is equivalent to "all that your brain can't perceive is unreal". Brain can't perceive where your tensions, worries and anxieties reside in your body. But you can't deny that worldly thoughts and anxieties disturb your mind.

A tree is hidden in seed, but brain can't see. Similarly, seeds reside in concealed form in a fully grown up tree, but your eyes can't see this. Surface reality is like the tip of an iceberg; while the existential reality is deeper and hidden, like the rest of the iceberg, beneath the sea water. The whole existence is difficult to understand for any brain.

Brain works on direct evidence to process and interpret sensory information from the nearby surroundings. It thus allows you to perceive and interact with world reality. While the brain is capable of incredible feats of cognition, creativity, and innovation, it doesn't have the ability to perceive which are subtle and belongs to fourth dimension.

The rules of mind are different from brain. The mind's distinctiveness is reflected in your thoughts, emotions and behaviors. Mind can carry you to your past lives by igniting your sub-conscious and unconscious part. Using only your brain is like focusing on the grass and missing out on the nearby forest. The mind is capable of seeing what your eyes can't.

During sleeping state, your brain enters a restive mode, and mind takes the charge of your body, and pull out your fear, dreams, and desires in the form of dream. It is during this time that your active mind creates the surreal landscapes with all permutations and combinations and weird scenarios that you experience in your dreamy state.

Man is a super-computer that acts as one collective machine capable of processing enormous amounts of data. The brain is focused on cognizing reality, processing information from five senses to build a coherent picture of the world around you. Its primary function is to help you navigate and interact with nearby surroundings, ensuring your survival and well-being.

You are whole; not divided (with brain, mind and consciousness). While the brain and mind are intimately connected, they have distinct roles and functions. The brain provides the foundation for your cognitive abilities, while the mind adds the richness, depth and complexity that make your life full of hope and aspirations.

In essence, your brain is like any other muscle that you have in your body. If you don't exercise it enough then it is prone to get frail. The brain is the lyricist of your world reality, while mind is the composer, adding melody and emotion to your experiences. For writing lyrics, you need words that come in brain. But music is emotion reflecting individuality and creativity.

Brain and Mind Works Together

You can't live without brain. And, you can't live even without mind. The mind is like a brother who totally relies on perceiving power of brain to know the surroundings. Brain can see, hear and feel things around you. It also remembers things, helps in the locomotion of the body and helps in minimizing error. But brain must not be allowed to dictate the mind.

For instance, famous world conqueror Napoleon was defeated in the battle of waterloo (1815) against Russian army. He made a blunder by taking a quick decision of invading Russian soldiers without realizing the biting cold and weather conditions of the battlefield. He lost the crown of "invincible". It was a loss which he could never recover.

Brain is merely data of collected information. If you depend solely on data and don't hear the voice of mind, you are bound to fail. Robert Falcon Scott, who prioritized data over mind's instinct, lead to his ill-fated Antarctic expedition. If you want to taste success in your chosen field, don't neglect the crucial role of mind in decision-making.

Brain thinks carefully prior to doing something or thinking of taking any action. Mind says it is always advisable to look before you leap. Acting without consulting the brain will lead one into endless trouble. It's like jumping into a river without judging its depth and current. In tough situations, the mind takes final decisions and brain merely gathers data and facts.

If brain is car, then mind is the driver. A car without driver is useless and vice-versa. Mind instructs the brain what to perceive and what to discard. Final decisions always remain in the hands of mind. It's the mind that really knows how to process thoughts, emotions and feelings efficiently.

For example, if you want to drive a car, your mind says "I want to drive a car!" and then your brain helps you put your hands on the wheel and legs on accelerator and brake. So, who thinks? It's your mind. Your mind is like the boss of your body, and your brain is like the helper. One must not let one's mind take a back seat.

Mind knows the skills and talent of the brain. Brain can acquire a car driving skill over a time. But what to do when emergency arises; only the mind knows how to tackle it. Brain surrenders in challenging situation. Suppose you are passing through landslide prone area, and inner voice comes within you to avoid that road, it's your mind that makes the decision.

The key difference between a strong mind and weak mind is that when life bombards one with storms, the weak mind fall and surrender himself to the fate but the strong mind will refuse to stay down defeated, rather he will try to rise up and swim amid the tides to emerge victorious. The strong mind will not leave the world as a loser but as a winner, a warrior.

The gist of this study shows that your mind and brain work together to help you do amazing things. Learning of anything that involves only brain results in only imitation. Mind filters all the gathered information to redefine you. By combining these amazing tools of your being, you can gain insight into your motivations, endeavors and passions.

You are not Mind

Mind is not everything as the saying goes. In emergency, you ought to take decision in a split of seconds, especially when you are hanging between life and death. While driving car speedily when brain observes that an accident is bound to happen, your intuitive power take the charge. The psychology of precise intuition involves no magic.

But still, one can't imagine life without mind. To think, to understand, to dream, to plan for the future you use mind as per your capacity and capability. To sustain life; to do various day-to-day works at home or at workplace, you need to use your mind. Remember, you are not the mind, just like you are not the body. Mind is just an instrument like eyes, ears, hand, mouth etc.

With mind, you limit yourself with fixed name, place and direction. Without mind, you are everywhere with no name and status. In deep sleep, when mind forgets wandering, you come nearer to your innermost being--you may call it 'Self' or '*Atma*' or pure consciousness. It also happens in Samadhi. But in deep sleep, you remain unconscious and miss the divine moment.

You may call yourself intelligent or brainy but you will have to admit that your mood and inner state (mind) are also important to you. You are mind (*manas*) and brain (intelligence) both at the same time. Brain perceives external and mind experiences your thoughts and emotions. The laws of the mind and the emotions are the same for everyone--spiritual or material.

For the inward journey, you need to transcend mind and intelligence. It means there should be no disturbance in the bottom of your consciousness. What happens then? Mind returns back to its source i.e. consciousness. Then mind and consciousness becomes one. This is the traditional approach of Self-inquiry by discarding everything in your physical existence.

Brain, Mind and Soul

Brain is the physical organ of neurons and synapses responsible for processing information of the outer world and helps in controlling bodily functions and stirring thought. It's tangible but scientific aspect of your existence. The mind is hypothetical concept which can't be located anywhere. It's the powerhouse of your thoughts, feelings and decisions.

What outer awareness is to brain; inner consciousness is to mind. It's the reservoir of your experiences, perceptions and embodied consciousness. The soul is independent of your mind, body and brain. If you want to experience your inner being, then you have to transcend your mind, body and limited consciousness.

Soul is the hub of everything in this whole existence including you. Mind is free to choose from material life or spiritual life. But you are not free from the result (*phala*) of your decisions. Brain makes you alert to your physical needs; while mind draws you towards desires. When you approach equanimity in your desire and need; you come close to your essence (Soul).

Mind goes on repeating the same thoughts; as there is nothing new in life. Everything is monotonous, everything is programmed. Brain collects the same data most of the time. Paramahansa Yogananda writes: "The soul is only a witness, it doesn't engage itself in the operations of human intelligence, mind and senses."

Every life comes with soul. Soul is nameless, formless and without support. Spirituality is not subject of either mind or brain, but of soul. The soul doesn't need any preaching or scripture to tell what to do and what to avoid because soul is knower of everything. It doesn't need your brain, body and mind to exist; soul is existence in itself.

Which is more efficient--Brain or Mind?

The brain moves faster than heart, but the mind moves even faster than light. Anything that moves faster can't be purview under the ambit of doubt. Bullet train in Japan runs at an amazing speed (200 miles per hour) with an incredible accuracy and interestingly, most of the time the train reaches at its destination in approved time.

You say this was an outstanding speed and accuracy because you compared it to metro train and *Shatabdi* Express. Compared to the speed of sound and light, the bullet train is mediocre. You made your judgment in common evaluation, where you consider two scenarios that belongs to different dimension. One is natural; and other is man-made.

No one knows the working of the brain correctly. No one understands how the mind thinks of unimaginable things. You compare two things with your conditioned mind. Mind serves the interest of no one except itself. Be real, don't be false. The problem is that one becomes deceived by his own assessment.

Brain can see the outside but can't turn inwards. It's your mind that knows your thoughts, feelings; your likings and disliking. Mind and brain both are your faithful servants. Brain finds it great difficulty in thinking out for itself, but having once accepted the mind as his master, it accepts everything that has been ordered to do.

Brain of all persons is almost same; but mind differs. Brain is master controller of your cognitive behavior, intelligence, motor control and personality expressions. It also plan and analyze current environment around you. Mind excels in emotional balance, innovative contemplation and shaping your social values and behavior.

There is almost universal agreement on the view that there is nature-defined specified task for brain and mind independently, and it depends on individuals how each hone the skill of their brain and mind separately. Some think slowly, while others take decisions quickly without any delay. Commandoes know how to take decisions swiftly after assessing the situation.

Thought is obligatory; it takes birth in every brain. But creative thinking is optional, you may use your mind or not. Everyone's brain is very soft with similar structure and function and message transferring via neurons also happens in similar way. But how mind analyze and interpret the collected data (through brain) varies from person to person.

The rewards and punishments, promises and threats are all in your brain. These are the burdens of your life. But mind adore a carefree life with bondage of none. These traits of mind help you to maintain balance in tough situations and instead of depending on your senses; one should utilize his intuition and instinct. By relying on mind, one can achieve success even in high-stress situations when everything looks topsy-turvy.

"The Self-created Lord has created the sense organ with the inherent defect that is by nature outgoing" (*Katha Upanishad*). Brain narrates the outer view and mind narrates the inner view. None is worthless. One can see the real world only when one has tested all possible conditions of life from the lens of brain and keenly observed it by the mind.

Key Points

- Brain is in your head. Mind is nowhere
- Brain is factual; mind is theoretical
- Mind is broadcasting stations for your feelings
- Attention and concentration are subjects of brain
- The faculty to suffer and to enjoy are powers of the mind
- Human brain memory capacity is 2.5 million gigabytes
- Brain can gather information through senses but can focus only one single at a time. If you are seeing an object with full attention, the mind wouldn't be able to sense information through other senses.
- Mind can sense an object and subject simultaneously. If you are hearing a melodious song, you can be aware of yourself also at the same time
- The power of the brain is mind itself
- If brain is knowledge; then mind is wisdom
- Mind has potential to release negative feelings and feel you relax
- Brain is ignorant of your true existence
- Only mind can turn inwards to the core of Reality
- Mind is the entryway to transcendental truth
- Feelings come and go like waves on the sea surface
- Thought forms should be uplifting
- Meditation is steady mind

~OM~

Chapter 3

Mind vs. Consciousness

Mind, body and intelligence are the objects of your outer world. They don't belong to you. In deep sleep, you remain alive but everything turns still and unmoving. But consciousness still remains vigilant even in deep sleep. The rareness of your consciousness is that there is no one in it but you. Mind or intelligence, no matter how closes to you, is still outside and doesn't fit into your essence. Mind means division in form of friend and foe; love and hate; life and death.

Whatever appears to be good or bad to you is mind. Whatever appears to be appealing or repulsive to your senses is brain. But when you go through "never before this" mystic experience is consciousness. This is not the experience of either mind or brain. This is the experience of empty pure mind. This is pure consciousness or witnessing consciousness. Brain is a fact; mind is a concept; while consciousness is presence underlying all your experiences.

A newborn child does not have mind but he has a developing brain with full consciousness. As the child grows and gain basic knowledge of his mother language; he begins to think, because thinking needs words. He learns from the nearby environment through his five senses (directly linked to brain). As a result, his mind and brain emerge as utilitarian tools for exploring and interacting with the world. His mind begins to expand; but his innate consciousness shrinks.

Mind is subtle form of brain; and the subtlest is consciousness. In the moments of zero thoughts, mind and consciousness becomes one. The mind is a thinking tool, while consciousness is the essence of human-being. The mind is a product of conditioning, shaped by experience, thoughts and emotions. Mind is a flux, constantly changing like clouds floating in the sky. Conditioned mind is influenced by external factors, and limited by its own perceptions.

- Consciousness is not a thought; but a presence
- Consciousness is not borrowed; but innate
- Consciousness is not a belief; but an experience
- Consciousness is not a sound; but silence
- Consciousness is divine; while mind is material

Consciousness is your Innermost Point

There is something in you that exist beyond the bounds of name, status and labels. It is unaffected by external environment. Consciousness is untaught wisdom and eternal flame of love. It is the unchanging, all-pervading awareness that underpins all experiences. It is the silent witness that observes all what happens in your mind without attachment or detachment.

Consciousness is the 'Self'. It is the attribute of soul (or atman). Mind resides within the consciousness. Mind only experiences whatever brain receives through sensory inputs and sends it. Consciousness is the experience of everything that is experienced by your bodily organs. "I" refers to the unchanging continuous element of your experience.

Consciousness means the sense of "I am". In a mind with empty thoughts you remain what is your deepest reality. Only in meditation, everything which is outside, which is accumulated from outside vanishes and only consciousness remains. You become the pure and simple essence of existence without any name, without any status.

Mind is contracted consciousness. Consciousness is more than that mind--it includes matter and intelligence too. R. Spira writes: "In ignorance, I am something. In understanding, I am nothing. In love, I am everything." Love that knows no rejection, no hatred, no jealousy, no lust....that is your ever-present nature that remains with you under all circumstances.

It's the mind which gives you the false notion of something like "I am so and so." Mind means thoughts. Your thoughts are borrowed, they are from outside. They have come to you, but they are not yours. Only the consciousness is yours and goes beyond the limitations of the mind. No one has given consciousness to you. It will remain with you even after death.

Mind is space of thoughts, reasoning and logic. Mind never remains fixed, but ever-changing. And, anything that changes can't be you. Consciousness is your intrinsic nature; your innermost point which remains at same point whether circumference of mind expands or contracts. When there are no clouds of thoughts in mind, still the sky exists. That sky is your Consciousness.

You can't understand the consciousness; until you become the master of your own mind.

Nature of Consciousness

Consciousness is the source and foundation of human beings. It is seen as Ultimate Reality in *Advaita Vedanta*. We are all 'conscious' in all states of mind--waking, sleeping and dreaming. Consciousness is a fundamental reality with no complicated theories, just bliss. It is contemplation catalyst for a thinker an insight inducer for seeker.

According to eastern philosophy consciousness (*chaitanya*) is not a focus of mind, intelligence or ego, but dwells in the Self. Consciousness is an attribute of the pure self, or the supreme reality. Mind is suppression, consciousness is liberty. Mind is narrowing process of your freedom. It can see everything, but it can look back at its source.

The opening verse (*sutra*) of Siva Sutras says that "*Caitanyam Atma*" It means consciousness is the attribute of soul (*atma*). Just like the light is the property of sun. You can't say that light and sun are same. In the same way, consciousness is the innate property of soul. When the soul leaves the lifeless body, there is no thinking or feeling within.

Buddha says: "The mind is everything; what you think, you become." But it's the consciousness behind the power of mind. Mind is nothing but consciousness. Intelligence is nothing but limited form of consciousness. Thought is something that begins and ends. Every time you are thinking of something to be observed. And, this is happening to each and every person.

You are surrounded by ocean of thought waves from all sides. Thoughts are subtle form of energy. The whole game of existence is among consciousness, mind, intellect, ego and soul. Right now, your consciousness is not pure, but covered with layers of dreamy dust. Mind, ego and worldly knowledge form stubborn dust around your consciousness.

The reflected consciousness operates through mind. And, the mind is inundated with all sorts of thoughts. Dreamy consciousness makes a wall between you and the Ultimate Reality. *Advaita* and *Tantra* firmly believes in the notion that internal organs i.e. *manas*, *buddhi*, *prana* and ego are only formations of your embodied consciousness (*citta*).

The dreamy consciousness and limited intellect is unable to experience the Ultimate. It is possible only in meditation (*dhyana*) and Samadhi, the higher limbs of traditional yoga. When one meditates, all impressions of the mind terminate and you become part of cosmic consciousness (*cit*). Expansion of consciousness turns it divine and pure.

Fighting with the mind or curbing thoughts forcefully is not a right approach. Learn to know thought patterns and feel its impact on your consciousness. By breaking the wall of 'I" consciousness, one rises above embodied consciousness and experiences oneness of consciousness. This is the state of supreme bliss and complete freedom.

There are various perspectives on the nature of consciousness. You may ask: Is consciousness a part of your body or is it something separate? Eastern philosophy ascertains that to understand the nature of consciousness is nothing but a subtle way to dig out layers of ignorance from your innermost being. But as long as mind moves in circles, your subjective truth remains a delusion.

Your whole life is always directed towards objective life. You can direct your attention towards the altering world; but you can't perceive at the source of your being. Sun is the source of all light and energy in this solar system. Similarly, consciousness is the underlying truth behind all thoughts, feelings and emotive behavior of a person. In *Bhavagat Gita,* Bhagwan Says:

अहमात्मागुडाकेश सर्वभूताशयस्थितः ।
अहमादिश्चमध्यंच भूतानामन्तएवच। ।10.20। ।

O Gudakesa, I am the Self residing in the hearts of all beings, and I am the beginning and the middle as also the end of (all) beings.

Let's see what western philosophers say about nature of consciousness:

Jean-Paul Sartre: "Consciousness is a being for which its own existence is at stake" emphasizing the existential aspect of consciousness.

Friedrich Nietzsche: "You must have chaos within you to give birth to a dancing star" suggesting that consciousness arises from inner turmoil.

William James: "Consciousness is a stream, changing continuously" linking consciousness to a flowing, dynamic entity.

Immanuel Kant: "The 'I think' must be capable of accompanying all my representations" stressing the unity of consciousness.

Attune Yourself to Natural Rhythm

In a fast-paced world, you give value to time-piece, but not to your inner clock. You eat your breakfast, lunch and dinner at fixed allotted time, not because you feel hunger because of your deep rooted habit. Your whole life has become mechanical and consequently everything is going out of your control. You are curious to know what is happening in world; but unaware of what is happening within you. Working like a machine without awareness is a symbol of being animal not a human.

Not your body but even mind knows well when to wake up and when to play; when to eat, and when to rest; when to awake, and when to sleep. But when you do any of these acts in excess or neglect; you lose the connection with the cosmic rhythm. Eating in excess or late night sleep hurdles the inner clock. Leakage of energy starts in regaining the natural rhythm.

Have you ever pondered why you sometimes feel uncomfortable or out of place in a peculiar situation? Your form is not the essence.

Mind is only reflection of your consciousness; and reflection is not the object. And, consciousness is only an attribute of "Self" (*atma*). Your essence is distinct from its gross and subtle manifestations.

You don't have experience of inner self because you miss unified rhythm in your mind, body and consciousness. Nature whispers secrets to those who are sensitive to the roots of their existence. Everything all around you has its own rhythm, and the world moves in cosmic rhythm. Change your weird state of mind into a balanced and rhythmic state of mind.

There is a natural rhythm everywhere--in your body, in your mind and in cosmic world. Your mind knows well what is the best time for sleep, rest, read or some creative hobby. Only a mind that is well aware about, what are you doing? can be your friend. When you attune yourself to natural rhythm of body, it attracts abundance, prosperity and good fortune.

The mind and the circadian cycle are intimately connected. Mind is accustomed to work by the time whether it's alarm clock or your own internal clock. If you want to be awakened at early morning, no alarm is as exact as your own inner clock. Just repeat inside your name and chant "you have to be awakened anyhow, no excuse no procrastination."

There is a natural clock in your genes and in every cell of your body. From bacteria to plants, from animals to humans, we all have so-called biological clocks that can anticipate the 24-hour day. Biological clock resides in the base of the brain. To harmonize your mind and circadian rhythm, listen what your body is saying silently.

- **Constant awareness:** You should remain aware of your true nature to achieve a state of bliss and calm undisturbed by external circumstances. Move your body like the rivers flow towards the ocean.

- **Feel happy and healthy:** Just like plants grow in proper manure, regular watering and exposure to sunlight; so let's listen what your body, mind and consciousness want to say and follow their beats. By synching with the natural world, you will feel more energy and more connected to the world around you.
- **Mental clarity:** The circadian rhythm affects mental clarity, focus and creativity, with most people experiencing peak cognitive function during the late morning to early afternoon. You will be able to complete your task effortlessly.
- **Hormone secretion:** Balance the sleep-wake cycle to regulates the release of hormones into the bloodstream by endocrine glands like melatonin (sleep), cortisol (stress), insulin (glucose) and growth hormone (growth and development).
- **Cardiovascular function:** Influences blood pressure, heart rate and cardiovascular disease risk.
- **Spiritual power:** Tuning your consciousness to cosmic vibration is the gateway to the inner world. It helps refining your divine power and you learn to remain calm and composed in adverse circumstances.
- **Electromagnetic field:** Enabling you to attract more cosmic energy, your body acquires magnetism. It absorbs universal energy and creates aura of its own, resulting in the expansion of electromagnetic field around physical as well as astral body.

Five States of Mind

If everybody is born with the same mind, why is it that some people become top scientists, bureaucrats, doctors or engineers and others miserably failed? There are many people who despite being blessed with all the available opportunities, still fail. The mind is the well-wisher to those who is calm, focused, mindful and ready to learn new skills.

Look at those who claim to be intelligent or genius! What is the sign of genius? It is confidence in their ability, persistent hard work, growth mindset and a quest for knowing more and more. A sleepy mind is like a closed book; it's worthless. He avoids mental effort, critical thinking and problem-solving--shying away from the hard mental work.

The world had seen Einstein as the most creative and productive mind since last century. But during his school days, he found class quite boring and dull. He was not at all satisfied with the education system of his school. In his opinion, classroom learning kills free thinking and new ideas. School education should be made inspiring and interesting to dull and sharp minds alike.

Any education system that discourages new ideas and creative thinking, it will produce only dull minds. If music, fine arts and sports are introduced, it can make students elated, ecstatic and extremely happy. During free time, Einstein used to play violin to feel relaxed, calm and free from all worldly tension.

Researchers and philosophers have applied diverse methods to examine the different states of mind. Mind can be calm, relaxed, confident and creative. On the contrary, the same mind can be anxious, negative, distracted and doubtful. The states of mind can shift and fluctuate, and its' a normal experiences to experience change in emotions and feelings.

You are conscious (only 1 percent), and remaining part of your mind remain unconscious. Osho writes in *Book of Secrets* "only one percent of the mind is conscious, and this one percent cannot win against the ninety-nine percent. It is going to be defeated. That is why there is so much frustration, because everyone is defeated."

Mind can be broadly categorized into five states as per Patanjali's yoga sutras (aphorisms)

Highly disturbed mind (*Kshipta*): Kshipta means highly disturbed and agitated mind. It can be compared to the monkey mind. Mind remains restless as it is directly linked to five senses. It's the senses which carry the mind to outer world. It happens as the mind is not trained to bring under the control of your unconditioned consciousness.

Even a normal person behaves as "*kshipta*" in adverse and challenging situation. His mind fluctuates like a pendulum of wall clock touching two extremes like love and hate; friend and foe; pleasure and pain; enthusiasm and boredom. To a fickle-minded person, decision making remains a puzzle and he seeks the advice of others.

Symptoms: restlessness, anxiety, confusion, lack of clarity, indecisiveness

How to overcome agitated mind?

Self-belief: Believe in yourself that you are part of all-pervading divine. Accept the weakness within you and try to take interest in your study or task in hand.

Cultivate positive thoughts: Allow your mind to remain with no thoughts. It will be like adding manure to the seeds of positive thoughts to express.

Be curious: Take interest in learning, explore new ideas and be acceptable to new thoughts and beliefs. Remember, God helps those who help themselves.

Pranayama & meditation: Yogic breathing helps you to be fully engaged in the present moment. Meditation instills creative and fruitful thoughts in mind.

Slow mind (*Mudha*): Dull, lazy and sluggish mind, although this one is better than the previous one. A person with dull mind remains worried, apprehensive and uncertain to take decisions. Most of the time, a "*mudha*" remains absent-minded. Absent mind is nothing but absence of awareness. He lacks motivation to carry out his dreams and aspirations.

- Learns slowly
- Forgets what he learns
- Trouble in perceiving complex subject
- Closed to new ideas or theories

There are many examples when a slow learner achieved something 'extraordinary in life. Great scientist Thomas Edison failed 1,000 times before inventing the first light bulb. By perseverance and have self-confidence, he overcomed all hurdles. He proved that intelligence can be developed and improved through learning, practice and non-tiring effort.

Unfocussed mind (*Vikshipta*): A mind that is easily distracted is known as butterfly mind or unfocussed mind. Mind never rests on solo object but swings between one object to another. Even the sharpest mind is dull at some moments. Similarly, even the dullest of minds can have a moment of perfection.

- Thoughts overpower the mind
- Feel helpless in tough situations
- Clarity seldom comes
- Only thinks, not act

All humans are influenced by three fundamental qualities of nature i.e. *sattva* (positive), *rajas* (dynamic) and *tamas* (potential). Unfocussed mind is doubt, it raises questions. Don't be afraid of unknown if you want to access intelligent mind. Embrace the unknown, and the unknown will become known. And, that's what happens to Madam Curie who discovered 'radium'.

Symptoms:

- Lack of concentration
- Feel a mental fog
- Get irritated easily

How to overcome:

- Engage mind in cognitive training
- Learning something new
- Play musical instrument
- Practice walking meditation

Focused mind (*Ekagram*): Mind is focused on one thing. It comes with regular exercising of mind and practice critical thinking. This mind is open to new ideas and ready to learn new things. Focused mind is problem-solving. Focused mind is like a super computer with fast processor, lots of storage capacity and easy to update.

The simplest way to cultivate this mind is: Whatever pleases your mind the most, indulge into it fully. It can be gardening, walking, playing etc. When a child plays with his toys, he forgets the whole world including his mother. This happens in focused mind.

- Learns quickly
- Understands easily
- Remember things

- Awareness goes deeper

Void state of mind (*Niruddha*): Totally stilled and serene mind where there no thoughts, only consciousness remain in your being. All the gunas (*sattva, rajas &tamas*) are neutralized. Duality eliminates in the void state of mind. When the awakened yogi sees the world as an expression of the inner divine Self, then the delusion of diversity disappears and he experiences unified consciousness. He finds Shiva both within and without.

- Supreme Void: Feeling of expansion with no boundary
- Fullness: No desire, no dreams; no past, no future
- Wisdom: Ultimate knowledge comes within
- Freedom: Transcend time and space limitation.

Mind is Ignorant of Consciousness

Consciousness remains a mystery, but then again so does mind. What is the purpose of life is still debatable. Dreaming mind can give many answers like attaining a respectable status in society; have an enough bank balance; owning a lovely family with caring spouse and beautiful children. But consciousness knows the ultimate purpose of life. Consciousness knows that everything is short-lived; limited to time and space dimension.

Consciousness knows the mind, but mind is ignorant of consciousness. In deep sleep, everything turns off, but not the consciousness otherwise you will die. It is the consciousness (*chaitanayam*) which illumines the mind and body. One can feel consciousness in his thoughts, bodily movements, and breath-movement and even walk. Mind cannot think about something which it doesn't know; mind can only think about something which it already familiar with it. Consciousness is unlimited and unbounded. Sleep happens to mind and body; not to your consciousness.

यानिशा सर्वभूतानां तस्यांजागर्तिसं यमी।
यस्यां जाग्रति भूतानि सा निशा पश्यतो मुनेः।।भगवद्गीता, 2.69।।

That Buddhi (understanding) which has the self for its object, is night to all beings, i.e., is obscure like night to all. But he, who has subdued the senses and is serene, is awake in respect of the self. The meaning is that he has the vision of the self. All beings are awake, i.e., are actively cognisant in respect of objects of the senses like sound. But such sense objects are like things enshrouded by night to the sage who is awake to the self.

A yogi in deep sleep remains aware. You may ask: how it happens when his mind, brain and intelligence turns completely still. It is the awareness of the consciousness; not the mind or brain. It is only awareness that functions even in deep sleep. At that time, whatever is false i.e. your name, position, background etc vanishes from your consciousness?

There is consciousness everywhere--it is in your body; it is in your mind; it is in your intelligence (*buddhi*); it is in your breath-energy (*prana*). Tantra says consciousness is in your gross body; in your subtle body; in your mental body; in your super-causal body and also in your soul. Mind is just the vehicle of consciousness to experience the life. Mind is only a part of your existence; and a part can't comprehend the whole.

The mind is like a river never remains the same, instead it is ever-changing. But consciousness is unchangeable. Consciousness is not restricted to mind and body as it exists apart from your mind and body. Medical science discloses that mind and consciousness are intrinsic in human-body. Physiology says mind and consciousness are related to brain's neurons.

Consciousness is the ultimate awareness that underpins all layers of your existence, and it has knowledge of the matrix of mind; psychology of mind; geometric patterns of thoughts. However, the limited mind which is an extension of consciousness is unaware of the true nature of consciousness. *Advaita* Vedanta also opines the similar views on mind and consciousness.

It says that ultimate (reality) can't be comprehended by mind or intelligence. Because it is covered by thought and *samskaras* as the mirror covered by dust and a fire is enveloped by smoke. *Bhagavad Gita* said very rightly--

धूमेना व्रियतेवह्निर्यथाऽऽदर्शोमलेनच।
यथोल्बेनावृतोगर्भस्तथातेनेदमावृतम्।।3.38।।

As a fire is enveloped by smoke, as a mirror by dust and as an embryo by the membrance, so are the embodied beings (The ultimate reality) covered by this desire.

It can only be experience in Samadhi when mind turns still and devoid of any thoughts. Buddhist philosophy says that there is veil of ignorance around mind and it can't see the true nature of supreme reality. Consciousness observes everything what you think or act without being entangled in them. The consciousness is everything; what mind thinks and what mind doesn't think.

--OM--

Chapter 4

How Mind Works?

The mind encompasses many functions and processing including perception, memory, thought, imagination, motivation, emotion, attention, learning and consciousness. Thoughts and feelings mainly come under the domain of brain which is composed of distinct components to execute different functions to exchange information in a hierarchical and integrated fashion.

People find it difficult to understand the idea of how the mind works. Mind works on two realms objective realities and subjective realities. In objective reality, world exists independently of what you think and interpret the objects of outer world. Subjective reality depends on what you think, feel or experience.

There are exaggerations made by the mind considering only the objective reality and ignoring the subjective reality. Subjective and objective are indeed distinct, yet interconnected aspects of human existence. Mind can't operate on its own strength, as it dependent on the subjective consciousness that illumines the mind allowing it to think, perceive and experience.

How you walk or talk; what you create through writing or inventing something new is all related to the functioning of your mind. The whole process involves various brain regions, neuron networks and neurotransmitters working together to define your thoughts, decisions and actions. Mind is capable of performing stupendous tasks that even super computer can't do.

The mind is endless space within you. Like a wheel, it can't function on its own it needs objects, thoughts, physical body, emotions, society, philosophical outlook to function optimally. Moreover, the mind of a child works differently from an adult and old age human. Mind can explore inner and the outer world if trained again and again.

Examining Thoughts & Experiences

Mind works through associations. It links new experiences to past indelible memories residing in your sub-conscious mind. Suppose a dog had bitten you badly in your childhood. And, whenever you see a stray dog chasing you in narrow lane the fear or anxiety from the past experience is generated. This is the example of associated memory ingrained in mind.

According to Jiddu Krishnamurti, "The mind is a product of conditioning, shaped by experiences, beliefs and societal influences." Strange are the ways of mind. The mind is a powerful vehicle that can be used for salvation or bondage. The mind seeks love, power, wealth in the outer world, and strangely also yearns for peace and freedom.

Amrita-bindu Upanishad says-

For man, mind is the cause of bondage and mind is the cause of liberation. Mind absorbed in sense objects is the cause of bondage, and mind detached from the sense objects is the cause of liberation. Therefore one who wishes to climb to Yoga must perform Karma Yoga consisting in the practice of detachment from sense-objects.

Actually, there is no solo yardstick to know the working pattern of mind. Undeniably, mind has always been an essential part of human development. It prepares you to survive in the outside world and establish an identity of your own as an individual. However, the truth is that mind represents a considerably broader dimension than you know of it.

To know the mind, first you have to know how the brain functions. They are complementary, they are not opposed. If one is there, the other is bound to be there, one can't exist without the other. The mind interacts with both brain & body, forming a composite coordination. Rene Descartes writes: "I think, therefore I am" that offers a new perspective of mind's nature.

Mind-Brain-body Interaction

There is intricate relationship between mind, body and brain. The world is composed of five elements viz. earth, water, fire, air and ether (space), and so is your body. Mind creates more worlds on the basis of past memories stored in brain. The five organs of perception i.e. eyes, ears, nose, skin and tongue receive signals as input from the outer world. These signals, which are the subtle perceptions of the gross world, stimulate the *tanmatra*.

Mind is an important of all your sensory experiences. Mind together with the help of sense organs experiences these subtle sensations as feelings. Body, mind and brain are also matter and they undergo continuous change due to the influence of external factors acting upon them. Change is the universal law of nature and only a rigid mind resist change. Immanuel Kant says: "The wise man can change his mind, the stubborn never."

Neuroplasticity: Whatever happens in your brain is reciprocated by mind. The mind shapes the brain's structure and function through new experiences, consistent learning and emotions. How brain feel in a peculiar situation and how the mind responds can help you to know the 'metaphysics' of mind.

Neuro-tranmitters: The common neurotransmitters in your nervous system are dopamine, Endorphins, serotonin and acetylcholine that facilitate communication between brain cells, influencing mood, thought and behavior. These chemical messengers can affect mood, appetite, anxiety, sleep, heart rate, temperature, aggression, fear and many other activities.

Brain regions: Despite a lot of discovery and research in medical science, there is still a lot to be discovered about the functioning of the brain. Brain is the hub of nervous system with different areas, such as the prefrontal cortex, amygdale and hippocampus, process various aspects of mental activity like decision-making, emotions and memory.

Inner and Outer Experience

Mind is the cause of your objective and subjective experience. It constantly process thoughts, emotions and experiences. When mind shrinks to the extent of non-existence, it becomes consciousness. And, when it expands to gross level, it becomes your elated ego. By knowing how mind works, one can understand consciousness, the moot centre of your existence.

By recognizing the mind's working pattern, one can know what bondage is and what liberation is and how mind is everything. The mind which is initially clouded by ignorance can be a stepping stone to touch the pinnacle of spiritual awakening.

Mind is not merely words, it's the sum total of what senses perceive, what brain interprets and how your impersonal side of your existence experiences the whole. Mind is divine and material both. A still, calm and unmoving mind is divine; while an egoistic mind is worldly. It is the psychology of mind that seeks to understand the workings of the human mind.

The hidden dimension of mind is unfathomable. When mind moves towards the objects, it takes the form of the gross object. But when the same mind turns inwards by curtailing all cognitive senses, it becomes subtle (more subtle than your '*prana*'). The mind's versatility and unpredictability make it both captivating and challenging to know how it works.

Mind vs. Computer

Computer work accurately and at high speed. The whole working process by which computer work is called 'automation'. In spite of stupendous success of computer in all branches of learning, still it needs detailed instructions from human beings to be able to operate. An individual human being sees things and does things with the mind relying on its perfection.

Mind doesn't work as computer process data based on binary code and algorithms. Mind works on many seen and unseen factors like brain capability to access information from surroundings, sharpness of senses in cognition, past impressions in subconscious and unconscious mind, environmental factors, social values and level of consciousness.

Mind is subtle matter which you can call neither inert nor conscious. It is in between your gross body and essential self. The light emanating from essential self (consciousness) is illuming the mind. And that light falls on sense objects that you perceive through five senses. Mind needs sense data to think, analyze and work.

If you check what is going inside the mind, mostly it is related to what your senses perceive. Your mental activity is based on the sense perception. And, what already exists in your unconscious mind is affecting your perceptions and decisions. Senses are powerful inputs that can either support or distract you from your desired goals.

T.o facilitate the understanding of the self in relation to the body and to highlight the merits of self-control, *Narada* in the *Bhagavata Purana* quotes the analogy of the chariot that is often used in the *sastras*. The body is compared to a chariot, the senses to the horses, the mind to the controlling reins, the sense objects to the roads to be traversed, the intellect to the charioteer, and the *Chitta*, the functions of the mind as well as the repository of all affections, to the binding cord. The ten *pranas* are seen as the axle tree, *dharma* and *adharma* as the wheels, the *jiva* bound by the sense of 'I' and 'Mine,' as the master of the chariot, the *Pranava* as his bow, the purified *jiva* as the arrow, and Brahman as the target.

If the charioteer is skilful and strong will-power, he can control the outgoing senses and withstand any storm" says lord Krishna in *Bhagavad Gita* (chapter 3, verse 41).

तस्मात्त्वमिन्द्रियाण्यादौ नियम्य भरतर्षभ।
पाप्मानं प्रजहिह्येनं ज्ञान विज्ञाननाशनम्।।

O best among the Bharatas, by controlling completely the sense-organs in the beginning [itself], you must avoid this sinful one, destroying the knowledge-action.

What is storm for one mind; it can be gateway to salvation to another mind. It all depends how one perceive and experience the world.

The mind's working is indeed multifarious, active and intriguing. Your perceptions and understanding of the world are shaped by individual minds, experiences and perspectives. The intricate interplay gives rise to the mind's remarkable abilities and quirks, making each individual's mental landscape unique.

Mind is a mix bag of joy and sorrow; union and separation; rigid and flexible. Like a fish, the mind can dive deep to navigate through the depths of thoughts and emotions with ease and fluidity. Like a bird, it can fly to soaring heights of creativity, insight and imagination. Like a cheetah, it can accelerate to incredible speeds of processing and reaction.

Mind has many moods and it behaves strangely in differing environment. Lush green grass evokes the smelling sense of mind and the docile mind start behaving like a donkey--sometimes be stubborn, reluctant to change and stuck in the same place of comfort. Or, like a smart crow, it can be quick in taking decisions and turning the table in its favor.

How Mind Thinks?

Thought is not located anywhere. A thought is how the brain cells interact and how they process the gathered information or data. The brain generates thoughts, emotions and sensations while the mind observes experiences and reflects on the subtle mental horizon. Mind is quite familiar with the brain patterns of thinking and learning.

Brain cells are dumb on their own, can't do anything much. An activity pattern of specific neuronal network set the brain cells in active mode. Brain cells or neurons are interconnected and interdependent like an 11 player's team in soccer. They need to work together to process any input and enable various nervous system functions.

Each neuron has a specific function to receive, process and transmitting data or information. Coordination activity of neurons enables brain to achieve some specific tasks in a stipulated time. It's like an orchestra where a team of instruments players creates soulful and soothing melody. A thought is not the music of single neuron, but a team of systemized neurons. It is like a bunch of transistor wiring. Sound is the output of this transistor made of wiring and some small sockets but these wiring system is not sun, sound (music) is there in atmosphere but due to this wiring system, transistor is become capable for producing the sound (music). Likewise in the case of brain and mind, consciousness is already present everywhere but due to the wiring of brain (neurons networking) the consciousness is able to express themselves in the form of thought (mind).

Information (or data) is all around us. Many people it all starts when your sense organs conceive something in nearby surroundings. Data is easily available and even business houses collect information from your surfing on your mobile or laptop. In essence, the brain collects information as per its potential and capability and the mind interprets and make sense of it.

Mind does data analysis and data correlation. Data is just a collection of syllables and numbers. You can measure data, but you can't measure the volume of your thoughts as it appears and disappears faster than you think. According to Freud, thoughts and emotions outside of your awareness continue to exert an influence on your action and reaction.

When you engage in creative or contemplative thoughts, only one thought yield fruits or result in something meaningful output (creativity). So, may be that thought outshines other remaining thoughts. You have so many tools of information nowadays to pick and choose as per your requirement and preference. You have smart phones, mobile devices, and the internet easily available but they may be constrictive not creative. Creativity is the ability to generate new ideas, concepts, or solutions. It is about originality, imagination, and innovation while Construction is the practical implementation of an idea, turning concepts into a tangible structure or system. Human intelligence remains superior in creativity, emotions, ethics, and adaptability compare to Artificial Intelligence (AI).

Ordinary mind loves to roam in external world. In order to access information from outside, your mind goes through the senses to gather worldly knowledge. If mind moves out, then whatever you know is mundane existence. But never merges information with a thought in mind. Having a thought means inner processing of mind—this is what is happening in mind.

You use information to filter your thinking process. Most of the thoughts run sub-consciously which makes it really hard to examine. So, let's zoom into the brain to check out what is going on when you think. When you have something interesting in your mind say a picture or an image or something like that you can see sharp and precise and switch very easily.

A computer easily calculates 3.4 billion times a second. Brain cells are comparatively slower and only do 500 operations in the same time at its maximum speed. Computer rarely makes any mistakes--a rough estimation is one error in a trillion operations. Brain is much error-prone and makes mistakes a billion times as often.

Brain is 99 percent self-oriented--most of nerve fibers never get outside of your skull. Brain cells never see what is going on in reality. Brain is sluggish, miserable and most of the time is self-centered and it still works. But you will be amazing to know that brain outperform computer in recognizing a face.

Brain can do amazing operations through a combination of sensory experiences, instinct and learning. Brain can do 20 to 30 or even 40 operations within a split second. Computer software needs many more steps, thousand and even million of steps to come to the same conclusion. This leads you to the fundamental principle of how human think.

Thoughts start taking its form with neural activity in the brain where information from senses, memories or emotions is processed. The brain recognizes patterns and connections between acquired information and accumulated knowledge. Brain doesn't distinguish between processing and output, because processing the information is the thought itself.

When mind is loaded with multiple thoughts at a time, this is not contemplation or concentration. Ordinary mind like an unchained horse can move anywhere as per his whims and fancies. A scientist or a research scholar thinking is linear, it goes straight. Even if he switches over to another thought, it has logical connection.

Mind Creates Elliptical Thoughts

Mind is not different from the thoughts. It is the inner space where thoughts appear and disappear many times. Mind is subject to modifications (*vrittis*) and fluctuations that are embedded in subtle thoughts that are invisible yet highly potent. The inherent defect of thoughts that mind generates is recurring. And, anything that repeats is boring and feels like a burden.

Mind is actually thought-producing process. If the thought-producing process stops, there will be no mind. If you watch the essence of all the thoughts, you will find that all new thoughts are reworked or updated version of an existing data. An exciting research by Dr Fred Luskin of Stanford University reveals that a human being can have around 60,000 thoughts in a day and 90 percent of these are repetitive.

Life is a cycle of repetition, where days and nights come by rotation. The sun raises from the same direction (east), sets in the fixed direction (west) and similarly breathes moves in and out in a predictable pattern. In the same way, you face similar challenges in day-to-day life, feel similar emotions (of love and hate) and think recurring thoughts.

Like a pendulum, the mind moves in two opposite extremes of love and hate; attraction and repulsion; materialism and renunciation; war and peace. When you love someone; hate comes naturally. Even a greedy person sometimes thinks of renouncing the world and donates his whole income to some charitable trust.

Tony Robbins writes: "The mind loves to repeat what it has already done, and it's hard to change the mind's habits." Mind is a link between any repetitive thoughts. Like a horse, mind tends to follow the same trails it has followed before. It is easy to walk on the familiar path, but it's sure that it may not bring any radical change in mind.

Mind resists staying in the present moment--the only path that is not repetitive. Past is repetitive; future is repetitive (in dream form) but present moment is just now. Mind thinks in terms of past or in term of future, but thinking process is not possible in the present moment. Thinking process happens in duality, and in the present moment there is no duality.

- Mind is thought-producing process
- It is loaded with thoughts
- Never remains the same
- Tendency of repetitive thoughts
- It's not easy to change mind's habit

However, there are simple ways to break the mind's tendency of repetitive thoughts. The first thing is awareness of what is going on in your time. While moving in outer world that feeds your all five senses, don't forget yourself. Suppose your smelling sense gives a signal of rose flower, don't bring your mind. Otherwise, mind will produce the same thoughts of past.

Learn something new whenever opportunity knocks at your door. Be trained yourself in playing any musical instrument like a guitar, piano, drum, violin etc. It gives something new auditory juices to your mind. Or, you can learn a new foreign language. Medical science says this is the easiest way to control dementia at the initial stage.

Travelling to new places can indeed ignite new thoughts, perspectives and ideas. It is a simpler way to break the daily routines, allowing you to break free from habitual recurring thoughts. The mind is merely an instrument of thoughts, but it can be exercise for contemplation and meditation. Of all the means, meditation is power tool for stilling the mind.

Breath and mind are in interlinked. It is fitting to focus mind on your breath. Breath comes and goes involuntarily; the only effort you have to make is breath-awareness. When you remain aware of your incoming and outgoing breath, thoughts starts disappearing and your mind comes in the present moment. When breath stops momentarily, mind comes to standstill.

- See nature without conditioned mind
- Learn new language for fresh insights
- Outing breaks habitual thinking
- Practice breath awareness

Mind can be Creative or Destructive

A solar light can be tapped for generating solar light, heating water, illumine road by installing solar light pillar or can be harmful in form of ultraviolet radiation. In the same way, mind can be used for new inventions or discoveries, solving mathematical riddles or can be used for creating prose, painting or positive expression. Otherwise, an untamed mind can be explosive.

Your thoughts are borrowed most of the time. They are not yours. Sometimes, thoughts are against you. You even disagree with your own thoughts sometimes. Be aware as soon as these destructive thoughts start floating in some space of your mind. You need to train your mind as early as possible. It will help you in clearing and cleaning inner space of mind.

Negative thoughts arise due to mind-fluctuations (*vrittis*). Don't let negative thoughts go down in your sub-conscious mind; otherwise it will bloom into your habit. Dacait *Angulimala* became a monk only after a strange encounter with Lord Buddha in the forest. He was earlier a brutal killer who used to wear a *mala* (necklace) made of chopped fingers of his victims.

If you think you are the owner of you mind or thoughts, you are making fool of yourself. Controlling mind is not a mammoth task if you bring your mind in divine consciousness. Practicing introspection is simple way to utilize mind for creation. Introspection is watching the thought-patterns--how thoughts are arising, thoughts are moving and thoughts are subsidizing.

Remember, what *Vedanta* and *Upanishads* says repeatedly that it's the consciousness which illumines the mind, empowering it to think, feel and experience the outer world. For an enlightened one, mind is the 'Self' (pure consciousness). You are neither thought nor mind. Experience this truth by regular "*dhyana*" (meditation). Effort leads to realization.

- Move with virtuous-minded people
- Spend leisure time in mindful walking
- Focus on the stillness between thoughts
- Don't identify yourself with any thought
- Believe in simple living & high thinking

Thoughts are voluntary or involuntary?

The scientists know very little about how and where thoughts come and what is the purpose of thinking. Thoughts, like air and food that you consume regularly, are external inputs that you needed to sustain life, rather than being generated solely by your mind (or brain). Your mind is more like receivers, filters and processors of external thoughts and ideas.

Thoughts have nothing to do with your mind, brain or intelligence. No doubt, thoughts come voluntary or involuntary within the mind. It can be labeled as good or bad; right or wrong; negative or positive; new one or repetitive. But don't forget that everything in life is impermanence, including your thoughts, emotions and feelings.

Mind is not a thought, but is the stage where thoughts walk, move, jump, dance and then disappear to let another thought to perform their act in distinctive way. The arrival of thoughts continues as long as breath remains in human-body. When thoughts work in associations, it is creative performance, while tearing and a disruptive thought makes your life hell.

Your mind doesn't contain thoughts within it. Language is the binding energy that makes you understand thoughts moving in mind. Thoughts are just a part of being alive. When you have a thought, neurons in your brain fire-up and create electrical impulses that tend to travel along a familiar pathway and create tiny chemicals called neurotransmitters along the way.

Every thought is energy; it has specific frequency. Thoughts trust in the energy of your subtle breath (*prana*). When your mind is clouded with hundreds of thoughts, you feel depressed. A scientist doesn't feel depressed, because his whole mind is directed to solo thought. That is known as contemplation (not weird thinking of ordinary mind).

Whenever a scientist starts exploring his contemplative mind, golden thoughts descend from the higher world. Great scientist Nikola Tesla once told: "My brain is only a receiver in the universe; there is a core from which we obtain knowledge, strength and inspiration. I haven't penetrated the secrets of this core, but I know that it exists."

The peculiarity of your mind is that there is no one in it but your own information. Mind is the treasure trove of information. That wealth goes on multiplying as mind adds more information with the help of five cognitive senses. Whenever you find yourself in complicated situations, this stored information helps you to sail your boat safely in stormy weather.

Thoughts come in mind both voluntary and involuntary. Your hidden desires, dreams, fluctuations (*vrittis*) are the cause of many thoughts. Some thoughts come from the universe that matches with the frequency of your mind. Your mind is just a receiver like your smart phone which receives signals from the satellite.

One may ask why thoughts not come in deep sleep? Your mind, intellect and senses being reduced to nothingness during sound, deep and dreamless sleep; and your consciousness comes nearer to the root cause of your existence i.e. "Self" (soul). Soul is formless (*nirakara*) and thoughtless (*nirvikara*) needs no support of any external world to sustain.

- Control distraction of mind
- Be aware of tearing thoughts
- Go beyond attachment & ego
- Cultivate focused mind
- Expand your consciousness
- Accept the cosmic intelligence

How Mind Works in Dream and Reality?

What is dream? And, what is reality? Mind can't differentiate between dream and reality (of awakening state). Professor Alvaro Pascual-Leone, a Spanish born at Harvard Medical School conducted a piano-playing experiment to two separate group--one who actually played and other who only imagined of playing piano.

The famous piano experiment was performed for two hours on five consecutive days. Their brains of actual performers and imagined performers were scanned every day. By exercising fingers muscles, it was discovered that region of the brain connected to finger muscles had grown beyond imagination. Interestingly, the motor cortex had expanded to both groups.

Thoughts come in mind in both ways--directly and indirectly. One volunteer group was actually playing the piano, and other volunteer group was only imagining of playing piano. In both physical training and mental training, brain responded in the same way. The mind is everything. What you think, you become.

Dreaming happens to you, you don't dream. Similarly, thinking happens to you, you don't think. So, the mind can't differentiate between dreams and reality. In dreams, mind thinks that whatever happening is real. The thin line between the dream world and the waking world raises fundamental question then what is the ultimate reality.

During REM sleep, the brain's neural activity resembles that of being awake, making dreams feel incredibly vivid and real. The mind's ability to create immersive, sensory experiences during dream can make it challenging to distinguish between what's real and what's just a product of your imagination.

The ambiguity is further complicated by the fact that your perception of reality is already filtered through your individual perspectives, biases and past experiences. The mind constructs your understanding of the world based on incomplete and subjective information, making it susceptible to misinterpretation.

The similarity between dream and reality has led some philosophers to suggest that reality might be just a collective dream or a simulation. This idea challenges your understanding of the world and encourages you to a question what is real and what is just a construct of your mind.

In spiritual tradition, the inability to differentiate between dream and reality is often seen as an opportunity for growth and self-discovery. By recognizing the fluidity between the dream world and the waking world, you can tap into the subconscious mind and access deeper states of consciousness.

Ultimately, the mind's inability to differentiate between dream and reality serves as a reminder of the complex and mysterious nature of consciousness. By embracing this ambiguity, you can cultivate a deeper understanding of yourselves and the world around you.

What is Reticular Acting System (RAM)

RAM receives input from your cognitive senses. It evaluates the input based on your prioritize tasks and interests. It is a delicate network of neuron or nerve cells in the brain that acts like a filter. It helps you focus on what is important and just ignore what's rubbish.

RAM helps you:

- Focus on what is vital
- Ignore rubbish information
- Prioritize tasks & stimuli
- Stay alert whenever needed

~OM~

Chapter 5

Individual Mind vs. Collective Mind

Individual mind is what you see yourself in the world inside you. It begins with your thoughts and feelings and ends in individual actions. Most of the human think that individual mind is everything. Think again! You are not the centre of the universe. There are many minds and many intelligence vast and deeper than what you think or observe. Collective mind is wider in its expanse and richer in its content.

Some hundreds years ago, the predominant tribal society was isolated and disconnected from others. With narrowed perspectives, isolated thoughts and beliefs, they missed the golden opportunities for connection and learning. Gone are the days when human tend to prefer living in cocoons. Human tend to work together whether they want to gain individual benefit or enhance the well-being of their community, or nation or of the entire world.

Collective mind and cosmic intelligence are often used interchangeably. Cosmic intelligence is priceless, selfless and has an edge over individual intelligence as it exhibits shared knowledge, wisdom and cognitive abilities of a group or community. It embodies timeless principles and patterns, unaffected by fleeting human thoughts and beliefs. It encompasses the interconnectedness of all things, revealing relationships beyond individual comprehension.

- Ordinary mind only understand duality
- It is limited in understanding
- Collective mind refers to integrated knowledge
- Collective mind denies division
- Accept the world wholly

Betterment of Society

The world has transformed into global village where the collective mind has the potential to work towards the betterment of society as a whole. With stupendous success in IT sector and social media platforms, people from diverse backgrounds can connect, share ideas and collaborate on a massive scale. You are not separate individuals, but interconnected threads in the collective tapestry.

Anything that is attached or relational is limited. Only universal is non-relational. If individual mind is bucket, then collective mind is bottomless well where you can make anything happen. Delve deeper into the well of knowledge, you will get as much as you can assimilate. Individual mind is limited experience in measurable time and space dimension. The limited is different from the universal mind which holds together the remotest parts of space and time.

In common parlance, mind is the process of paying attention that requires focus and intentional effort. What you think, observe or contemplate are the impressions of mind. Your individual mind is your personal subtle property--related to personal thoughts, imagination and perceptions. No one except you can access what is going on in your mind. In broader sense, you remain cut-off from the infinite working of the world.

The universal mind is not the mind literally, it is the ground of all human mind; the ground of both knowledge and experience. The collective mind or universal mind is boundless and all-encompassing. The moment of subduing individual mind is the gateway to cosmic awareness. The mystery of human existence lies not in individual mind, but in finding something that includes all existential minds.

You don't see things as they are, but what your empirical mind reflects back to your consciousness. Most of the trouble in the world is caused by individual mind that has limited access to information and knowledge. It divides you, feeds your ego and makes a wall between you and the wisdom. Universal or collective mind transcends the individual mind.

Mind has a different meaning, depending on the circle of consciousness you are in. If your mind is moving in the universal dimension, the bigger your consciousness' circle will be. If the mind is contracted, the smaller your consciousness circle will be. Bhagwan Ramana Maharshi used to say: "Mind is consciousness which has put on limitations. You are originally unlimited and perfect. Later you take on limitations and become the mind.

Nature of Individual Mind

Individual mind is nothing more than your own experiences (good or bad) in specific time and space. Your body is part of nature. Normal mind is skeptical mind. With this physical body and limited senses, you can have the limited mind only. It will give you the feeling that you are separate entity with peculiar name, family background, status and economic status.

The creative work is best done by individual mind in calm and peaceful environment. To develop fresh and creative ideas, you need to be cut-off from the society for a while. Then, what you experience is your individual. J. Krishnamurti says "It's beautiful to be alone but I want to add one more sentence, "To be alone doesn't mean to be lonely". It means the mind is not influenced and contaminated by society." Be in society, work for society but your mind should not be influenced by society. In this case your will be alone but not lonely.

Individual mind is unconscious. There is lack of self-remembering; although it is filled with egoistic thoughts. It loves dreaming; but abhors mindfulness. It can never stay quiescent. It contracts your consciousness and binds your soul. Whatever individual mind thinks and feels translate it into action without looking at the consequence.

All individual minds share one thing in common: projecting the inner feeling on others. A normal human always speak and act out what his mind instruct him. If you have a negative feeling, like hate, anger, jealousy, you express that feeling through negative thoughts, negative actions and negative talk. This has a deep impact on your life.

The basic nature of mind of an individual one is same for everyone--whether you are spiritual or material or mixture of both. The individual mind is egoistic, self-centered, undisciplined, doubtful and easily distracted. It never listen to the unconscious; the secret whisper of the divine. Instead, individual mind tend to concentrate on problems, worry and anxiety of life.

The common mind live in moods not is presence. He is worried for the future and feels nostalgic when past memories linger on the mind. He does not know how to maintain balance to their family life and professional life. He doesn't know when to say 'yes' and when to say 'no'. He doesn't know how to earn money and then how to spend wisely.

Mood swings is natural part of individual mind experience. Good feelings go with positive thinking and bad feelings go with negative feeling. Emotions and moods fluctuate due to hormonal changes, pleasing or unpleasing experiences, relationships, social interactions, tearing thoughts & perceptions and also physical health and well-being.

You live in your mind. The feeling of incompleteness will remain creep within you. Mind presumes that by accumulating wealth and gaining power you will be complete. But all these satisfactions are fleeting. You have identified yourself as gross form that is basically concerned with the objective world. Whatever happens in outer world create ripples in your mind.

Collective mind is universal, but your thoughts are personal. Thoughts shouldn't be allowed to make a wall between you and the universal reality. Shiva instructs every seeker to be wave-less (*nistarang*) before practicing any meditative practice for knowing the ultimate truth. Even in your manifested form everything changes with changing world, but centre remains the same.

There are two obstacles to know the divine wisdom: one is ignorance of its existence and second is stubborn mind reluctant to open. Align your individual mind with the cosmic mind that exists within your experience and that throbs at the heart of the entire universe. It helps you to deconstruct the false constructions of the mind, and reveal the true wisdom.

Siva Sutras (aphorisms) clearly indicates that you are not mind, but silent and still consciousness. Accept the collective mind as you accept your individuality. A verse "*drisyam sariram*" (1.14) from this scripture reveals that manifested world is not different from your pure consciousness. Perceive your body as you perceive the world.

- Mind moves in familiar path
- Mind is obstinate & unmoving

- Don't be upset over trivial things
- Change old pattern of thinking
- Accept unified mental state

Nature of Collective Mind

An average mind appears to think that his ideas and thoughts are peerless and ultimate; and needs no correction or rectification. A disciplined mind thinks that the life is a training ground to learn 'new' every-day. A research scholar considers his life to be a laboratory and to an enlightened one the whole minds belong to one Supreme. While others takes the life to be a non-ending process of give and take, and are eager to exchange the knowledge with others.

It is human nature to know and inquire what is happening in outside world. A desire to connect with and learn from other is intrinsic in every mind. This is the reason why great explorers Christopher Columbus and Vasco da Gama discovered new land in a bid to connect with unfamiliar cultures. Their enthusiastic voyages marked significant milestones in human history, added information of other lands and the mindset of other people.

Exploration and discovery are vital aspects of human mind, leading to growth, understanding and a deeper appreciation of shared knowledge that what you call collective mind. The collective mind is largely additions of vast, ever-evolving repository of human knowledge and experience. To add terrestrial knowledge, astronauts and space agencies like NASA are constantly in space mission programs to discover potential life beyond earth.

Collective mind is like a big circle of learning and growing together to understand the world better. The thought of adding new things feels great to humans. Here, additions refer to either new ones or repairs or better replacement of existing knowledge and experience. The idea of earth is stationary and sun is moving around the earth was considered to be true. Now, it has been discovered that it is actually the earth is moving, while sun is stationary.

The collective mind is like a big group of people contemplating together. The whole collective process invites new thoughts, fresh ideas and pragmatic perspectives. It represents the shared reservoir of knowledge, experience and wisdom of humanity. By tapping into it, you can accelerate your personal growth and become a more informed, empathetic and enlightened individual. In collective mind, the whole mind comes within you.

You have to be aware of the way you present your thought to be people and need to ensure that they are not misunderstood. Your individual mind is not really individual, deep down it is collective. Your mind and my mind somewhere deep down is one. The collective mind represents the shared reservoir of knowledge, experiences and wisdom of humanity.

Man cannot survive with relying upon someone. He has to look up to somebody for guidance and peace. Without love and understanding for the people around the world, little value can be given to unified mind. Such activity dilutes one's ego and creates a feeling of oneness. In essence, you can say that the collective mind represents a bridge between man and divinity.

Connecting with global unity can indeed grow your mind by:

- Maintains curiosity and an inquisitive mind
- Bringing your presence into this world
- Accessing universal knowledge and ideas
- Understanding different emotional aspects of life
- Learning from others' experiences

- Expanding your knowledge bank

Artificial Intelligence and Collective Intelligence

All the information that humans have in this world is part and parcel of individual mind and collective mind. For a human to have this whole information in his mind is almost impossible. Whatever you know is not enough, you have to brush-up your knowledge. As more information is adding each day, so cosmic mind keep growing. Cosmic mind is collective unconscious, where individual minds tap into a universal, interconnected web of thoughts and ideas.

Artificial intelligence or AI is machinery works by combining data, algorithms, computer system and machine learning. AI is manifestation of collective intelligence, where hardware and software components systems connected to World Wide Web (WWW) together to create a more intelligent whole. It is mainly used in robots, route navigation, image/sound recognition.

AI works by leveraging complex algorithms, computing power and data to enable machines to learn reason and interact with humans and the environment. There is a need to build a global digital platform for collective intelligence. Traditional Knowledge Digital Library launched in 2001 is an Indian government initiative to preserve and protect traditional knowledge and cultural heritage. The purpose is to develop collective intelligence that benefits humanity.

The human mind is conditioned one by society, education and family background. The ordinary mind learns to see things the way society has chosen to see them. The most foundational principle behind collective thinking is diverse. We have diverse minds, so what you perceive any object can be different what I perceive the same object. Collective thinking bridges the gap between you and me. In a way, what you miss, I observe it and vice-versa.

Intelligence working together in nature is known as collective intelligence. Bird-flocks and fish schools are good examples where same species work together. It is in nature where you watch ants making trails that are like super-highways to access the food sources. Other example is group of insects build huge termite mounds like 10 meters high in Australia and Namibia.

Indian philosophy reveals that mind, intellect and ego are subsets of consciousness. These inner instruments (**अन्तःकर्ण : मन-चित्त-बुद्धि-अहंकार**) are subtle and intangible in nature. Mind may differ from individual to individual, but deep down all minds are interconnected. Collective intelligence is emergent phenomenon where groups of people process information in achieve an insight that is not understandable by an individual member of the group.

How Collective Mind Gains Knowledge?

'Conscious mind' this word may seem very attractive but the collective consciousness is hidden somewhere in the lower unconscious mind. To enhance your creativity and insights, you have to tap into the collective unconscious. Medical science is now admitting that the cause of many diseases is not physical, but deeper and hidden layers of your mind.

The world of today is very different from what it was a century ago. You have moved beyond the first-hand knowledge of the world that what you perceive or observe individually, which gives you multiple points of view of looking at the world now. Be it medical science or rocket science, the experts are zooming their subject of knowledge from all possible angles to dig out secrets that remain hidden for many centuries.

Integrating information is an intriguing concept that sparks imagination and exploration of the collective mind's potential. The great advance of science, in its numerous branches, has changed the world beyond all recognition. It explores to the bottom of the unconscious psyche to access accurate data (without error or negligible error).

Collective mind is coming together of many minds without losing individual mind's liberty like never before. Change is not necessarily the rejection or denying of the past; it is only an attempt to mould and modify the old ways of life and thinking to new conditions. And stagnation means death and decay.

Collective mind is consolidated and unified one and it's understanding is greater than the sum of its individual parts, leading to a more comprehensive and nuanced comprehension of complex topics.

A collective mind understands something new task through:

(a) Every idea counts: Individuals contribute their unique perspectives and information to reach the maximum potential of understanding something new (idea or thought etc). Every persons matter and every idea counts in shared knowledge.

- Every individual's idea counts
- Each perspective adds value
- Individual contributions make the group stronger
- Diversity of thoughts creates a deeper understanding

(b) Distributed cognition: When the task is big, it's better to divide cognition among members of the group to solve the complicated problem. The groups combined cognitive abilities process and analyze information. The distributed cognition allows:

- Many minds work together as a team
- Shared understanding to emerge
- Problem-solving attitude emerge
- Invites innovative solutions

(c) **Social interaction:** Man is a social animal, and he can't live in isolation. Collective mind can be harnessed for deeper understanding by integrating different valuable opinions on the same problem. Knowledge expands to higher dimension when members contribute and share ideas to make data bank richer. Individual is limited by ignorance, because no one is complete. Members interact, discuss and build upon each other's ideas.

- Judge with maximum amount of data
- Think in long-terms
- Create fresh ideas
- Understand each other better

(d) **Feedback loops:** Understanding is a map. Each of our mind's maps differs. Feedback loop see inside and outside of every individual idea. It helps in identifying what is leading you into wrong misinterpretation. Feedback loops are vital in correcting mistakes, repeating some information or idea, thereby making the understanding more powerful and meaningful. The group refines its understanding by mutual approval and acceptance.

(e) **Pattern recognition:** Pattern recognition is a means to dismantle puzzling blocks and support clarity of mind. It is like connecting dots to see a hidden picture. Each person in the group has few original ideas or thoughts. The collective mind of that group identifies connections between distinct thoughts and ideas. The collective mind identifies patterns and connections across individual contributions.

- Line up the possibilities in connecting ideas
- Linking the information from different sources
- Recognizing shapes or structure in data
- Understanding flows freely

(f) Working coordination: Synchronization at all levels of working structure would be required more as the world advances into new digital revolution. Adaptive learning advocates a working coordination among all participants aiming for united cause. The collective mind adjusts, aligns and updates its understanding as new information arises. It aims at strength and solidarity as the strength of a chain being the strength of its weakest link.

How Individuals Contribute to Collective Thinking?

Individual mind is the breeding ground of ego, attachment and repression. But interestingly, it is a part of collective mind. There is no limit to the powers of minds when they unite for single cause. By distributing particular task to each mind, the collecting mind works wonders to make the group stronger, reliable and trustworthy.

Perfection in any task can be attained only when every individual gives his/her maximum potential. Individual actions make a big difference in collective thinking. Collective thinking helps spread useful and progressive ideas and research in various spheres. The team has a better chance to complete task undertaken in less time, less energy and less to fear of failure.

Collective thinking can't exist as an individual; instead it inspires unity and collaboration of various minds instead of working against each other. It helps in sharing knowledge relying on each other's thoughts and ideas and together they create something marvelous. Individuals contribute to collective thinking in many ways:

- **Being creative and unique:** The happiest part of creative thinking is that every individual shares his/her ideas and opinions to grow and adapt together. Sharing ideas has always been an essential part of human development. It helps you to excel in the outside world and establish an identity of each individual. Each member of the collective team brings their unique experience and thoughts to the group

- **Removing listening barriers:** Collective thinking calls for good listening skills. Listening is a process that calls for unbreakable attention. Listening is to be understood as the total process that involves hearing with apt attention, being observant and making interpretations. Others listen, understand, and add to these ideas creating a snowball effect.
- **Clearing doubts:** As you rest firmly on your own faith and opinion, in collective work you allow others equal liberty to stand by their own faith and opinion. Individuals ask questions, clarifying doubts and encourage deeper thinking.
- **Team-spirit:** People with specialized knowledge share their insights, enriching the collective understanding. When a mighty log of wood floats down a stream, it carries on it dozens of birds and doesn't sink.
- **Providing perspectives:** Individuals offer diverse viewpoints, helping the group see things from different angles. You must know where to draw the lines between the right and the wrong.
- **Encouraging others:** Individuals support and motivate their peers, fostering a collective environment. It helps you stay connected and focused, making your work more enjoyable and meaningful.
- **Positive thoughts:** If seeds are not planted in vacant field, then nature fills it with grass and weeds. In the same way, if positive thoughts are not generated in mind, then it is replaced by negative thoughts. Working in team helps you to generate promising thoughts that help connect the dots between ideas, revealing patterns & relationships.

- **Activate reasoning:** Observing others' reasoning processes and thought-patterns enhances individual reasoning skills. Individuals reflect on the discussion and summarize key points, ensuring everyone is on the right track.
- **Error detection:** Thomas Edison once said: "Mistakes are the stepping stones to success." But same mistakes should not be repeated. The importance of collective effort and unity in overcoming challenges can't be ignored. Collective thinking helps identify errors in the nick of time and rectify it at the right time. It promotes accurate and significant conclusions.

Understanding Your Own Mind

As I said earlier, the laws of the mind are the same for everyone. Like laws of gravitation, it is universal in nature. Mind identifies itself with the stream of thinking. Thoughts roam either in past or future, but never rest in the present moment. Mind has innate tendency to run after the mad world of name, fame and money. It indulges in finding fault in others.

Like any person, you can think any kind of thought at any time. There is no restriction. Every mind is filled with positive thoughts and positive feelings; negative thoughts and negative feelings, and so is yours. In individual mind, desire and creativity exist. If you want to rewire the old connections, focus on the inner and consciousness will take care of the outer.

Your mind is your world of dreams, desires, knowledge, feelings, emotions and experiences. The capacity to question, to analyze and to understand is a property of individual mind. Privacy is power. People cannot destroy what they do not know. Others don't know what wealth is lying in your personal world. Collective mind is mixed ingredients of all experiences.

All minds are same to some extent. It is formless and subtle in nature. It is fountainhead of your inner world of thoughts, emotions, and feelings. Thought is like a seed with potentiality of becoming a tree. If you take proper of seed, Thoughts move constantly like ever-flowing stream; and rests only during deep sleep.

No matter whatever you are doing, stay connected to the content of your thoughts. If negative thoughts surpass the positive thoughts, you need to be aware more. This thinking must be undone. To understand the collective mind, start by understanding your own mind.

Nature of mind: Mind can be caring, loving, empathetic and generous. Or, it can be a house of anger, jealousy, hatred and tearing thoughts. It depends upon "*samkaras*" (past life impressions). Embracing spirituality in life helps in freeing mind from all bondages. It makes you sensitive and aware of your own mind and other people's behavior.

Feelings and emotions: Relationships can't last long with moods and conditions. It is maintained by feelings. Positive thoughts carry positive feelings; while negative thoughts carry negative feelings. When purified thoughts and positive feelings are combined together, then a sort of miracle happens, your understanding and energy expands like never before.

Mind-body relationships: Mind can't exist without body and vice-versa. Mind and body are complementary to each other. The happiness of your life depends upon the vigor of your body and the quality of your thoughts. Law of attraction states that like-minded attract each other; and unlike one repel. So, think positively and treat your body like a temple.

Attitude Matters: Many people fail in life owing to the habit of delaying or procrastination. It makes your mind weak, dull and unimpressive. Make the habit of doing things at right time whole-heartedly. Famous Persian poet says "When you do things from your soul, you feel a river moving in you, a joy."

~OM~

Chapter 6

Types of Mind

Every child is born with pure consciousness (with no mind). But as he grows older and mature, his mind is manipulated by thoughts, beliefs and assumptions. Mind as a seed has the potential to become another Tulsidas or Shakespeare; J. C. Bose or Einstein. But few of minds change their childhood dreams into reality. It's really amazing!

Perception of mind changes at every turning phase of life. Remember, mind is responsible for your success or failure in life. It changes its color like a chameleon. A highly conscious person remains vigilant of the acrobatics play of the mind. But ordinary mind is stubborn. If mind is rigid, biased and closed to new ideas, you remain at the same condition throughout the life.

Medical science reveals that all human beings are 99.9 percent are identical in their genetic make-up. The mind is 'individual' in you. Individuality is not in your physique or complexion. It's the mind which defines your personality, your attitude and your likes and dislikes. Your mind shapes your actions, and your actions reflect your peculiar thoughts, beliefs and experiences.

Behind most of your actions and choices, mind is always the deciding factor. Mind seeks happiness and its meaning varies from person to person. A Buddha-like mind is ready to renounce kingdom for the sake of truth. Hitler-like mind is ready to go to any extent to kill innocent people mercilessly. A devotional mind of Kabir and Nanak sees divinity everywhere.

And when happiness is the sole objective of mind, it assumes many shapes and color as per the taste and temperament of your sub-conscious mind. Just like fingerprints, minds are unique to each individual, shaped by their past impressions (*samskaras*), family environment, educational background and friends circle.

Face is the mirror of the mind. A contented mind feels the satisfaction whatever life offers him/her. He never feels dissatisfied and tumult. A child-like mind conceives world as a playground. He looks at the world with curiosity. A fearful mind remains tense and worried all the time, and his face radiates the inner feelings.

Old Mental Impressions in Mind

There is old saying in India that taste of water changes every two miles and language changes every four miles (**कोश कोश पर बदले पानी, चार कोश पर बानी**). Although, water is colorless and tasteless by nature, but human experience different tastes of water in different places owing to differing concentration of the total dissolved minerals in the water.

In the same breath, mind is empty by nature. John Locke gave a statement that "A child is born like a blank slate and its later behavior is shaped by experience." But Indian philosophy says a child is born with old mental impressions (*samskaras*) that remains hidden at early stage. But as he/she grows, it makes an impression in the conditioning of his/her mind.

Like water, mind is dynamic and adaptive in nature. Stagnant water can be compared to dull and slow mind that is reluctant to learn and flow. Water flowing in turbulent river can be compared to adventurous mind which is bold, daring and open to new experiences. A smooth flowing river represents a disciplined mind that is focused, clear and open to new ideas.

Some children have sharp mind and they learn very quickly whatever is taught at the classroom or imparted by his/her parents at home. Swami Vivekananda showed his mind's inclination towards monastic life since his childhood. Great mathematician Ramanujan showed his genius mental strength at his early school days.

Power of Attention

In many circumstances, you might have found yourself helpless, victims of challenging time. Why you feel helpless and regretful when failures comes in your life. Why you remain ignorant of the hidden power of attention and concentration within you. Make your destiny by fully engaging your mental faculties. Don't forget that you are the producer and director of your life. You have the capability to turn the table in your favor.

Life is not a bed of roses. In every step, one has to struggle for making his or her place. Those who are determined and optimist are rewarded with wonderful feat. And, all it depends upon how you use your mind in tackling the complexities and nuances of life. A mind adorned with an apt attention, emotional intelligence and adaptability can change everything odd or even in his favor. It's up to you how you can use these skills to bring revolution in your life?

As I mentioned earlier that every person is born with a blank slate; but some have curiosity to learn more and they avail every opportunity to embellish their mind with poetry, or with music, or with art or with classic literature. The main difference between genius minds and dull minds is the difference in their power of attention to be filled with experiences and wisdom. Compare the dull with the genius one. The difference is in the degree of attention.

Life phenomenon is same, but everybody experiences it differently. Because of this fact, everyone thinks, acts and reacts distinctly. On a social level, your mind has implications for how you approach issues such as opportunities waiting for you and stumbling-blocks in the path of development. On an individual level, your thoughts and actions have a deep impact than you may realize. It creates room for unique perspectives and independent thought.

Everybody knows something about attention. You see its results every-day. Man is bestowed with the power of attention. A brilliant mind can learn things and can keep them in his mind. But dull mind lack this power. Stupendous success in art, music, literature etc is the outcomes of consistent practice with devotion and dedication.

Everybody's mind becomes attentive at times. It is believed in many cultures that new moon ensures clear thinking, focus and heightened awareness. You all become attentive spontaneously upon those things you passionately love or admire. Dull mind cannot be attentive upon anything long at a time. They constantly forget what is told to them.

"The kingdom of fools is ruled by the wisest fool" as old sayings goes by. Remain in the company of wisest fellow, and avoid the company of fools. Mind has tendency to waste the time in idleness. The mind is like the tail of a dog, you may draw it straight as long as you please, but the moment you let it go it again becomes twisted. Wisdom helps you to achieve many things in life while foolishness brings only failure and rejections.

The efficient use of your mind enables you to grow and evolve and make right decisions at the right time. It will be effortless exercise to pursue your passions and interests and touch the maximum potential of your mind. Otherwise, frugal use of mind can lead to stagnation. Furthermore, research on mind has revealed that by enduring learning, critical thinking and self-awareness, you can unlock your full potential and make the most of your mind.

Mind is trouble-free by itself. You are what you think. Whatever you think constantly, you attract more of that into your life. It is you who make it tensed mind, ferocious mind or cunning mind. If you yearn for peace, success and freedom, learn to control your mind. Then, thoughts automatically come under your unconscious mind. Practice meditation to tame your mind. Ensure that you are turning your thoughts sublime, transparent and divine.

In the nutshell, one can enhance his power of attention by:

- Embellish your mind with creative thoughts
- Have a strong faith in yourself
- Be yourself, don't imitate others
- Hear inner wisdom in tough time
- Accept the challenges in life
- Learn from the failures
- Be open and curious to learn new

Why Mind Differs from Individual to Individual?

Every individual is different not in terms of physique and looks; but also in capability of thinking. Thinking is not a science that can be learnt from merely textbooks, but it can be absorbed a little at a time, and that the absorption process can go on life-time. Thinking can be positive or negative according to the nature of thought-constructs (modifications of mind).

No two people think in the same pattern, and that's what makes the world interesting. The world is vast spectrum of human minds, showcasing the unimaginable diversity of thoughts, emotions and characteristics. Cheerful and gloomy; genius and dull; divine and evil--this contrast underscores the complexity and uniqueness of each individual's mind.

Relationship runs on the wheels of attachment and aversion. It's your mind that holds the key to your relationship to the outer world. You create your experience through your inner language. You know that if you act out of negativity, it will have negative effects. If you are furious and you interact with people, you will communicate anger and creative negative effects. As the seed, so is the fruit.

When learning is enticing, its volume doesn't register on one's consciousness. If you have learning and curious mind, than you can learn quickly by analyzing information, process the information efficiently, communicate effectively and comfortably adapt to new situations. A dull mind seldom can work efficiently. They are most interested in themselves. If they are stuck in this thought-pattern, let them go.

Most of your dreams and desires come from conditioned mind and impulse. You chase after those things that appear to be exciting to you. Everyone is responsible for the nature of his/her mind. A calm and serene mind stay determined and focused on the goals. A turbulent and chaotic mind can't control his thoughts, emotions and actions. Like waves, minds ebb and flow, shaped by the tides of experience, thought and emotion.

Mind perceives that reality which is ever-changing. Reality for you is your mental activity. Someone who is courageous, confident, adventurous and authoritative have lion mind. And, the one who is curious, loyal, affectionate and joyful have dog mind. Like the ancient Chinese symbol (Yin and Yang) mind represents the harmonious existence of opposites.

"*Jnanam Bandhah*" (Shiva-Sutras) preaches that worldly knowledge which is accumulated from functioning of mind and senses infused with illusion (*maya*) are the source of bondage. In simple words, you can say that mind is bondage, but it is also a means to liberation. A timid and fickle mind is bondage; while a transformative mind is freedom.

Whatever you experience is mind. It is the open book of your experience that includes all thoughts, memories, moments of intense happiness or sadness, bodily sensations and outgoing sense perceptions through hearing, touching, tasting, smelling and hearing. If you move in pious company, your religious mind cultivates. While mingling with bad company, the same mind catches dirt. Like classic tale Jekyll and Hyde, in mind good and evil co-exist.

'Mind is all' for worldly person; and 'mind is nothing' for a monk or hermit. Mind depends on five senses in perceiving the world. Without mind, senses can't perceive the world on its own. Higher than the senses are the object of sense; and higher than the objects of sense is the mind. Mind is powerful than the senses. A monk can control his senses and mind at his will.

Even the mind of a monk wanders, but he is aware of it. It is not possible for those who never have any conception that mind can lead you to success. Once you fix your mind on your goal, put your heart and soul into it, then no one can stop you. Your mind is free to make any decision or desire you wish. But you are not free from the consequences.

Mind is the organ of conflicting or differentiated thoughts. Mind works on the basic principle of sensation and response. There are nine *rasas* namely erotic (*srngara*), the comic (*hasya*), wrathful (*raudra*), the compassionate (*karuna*), the disgusting (*bibhatsa*), the terrifying (*bhayanaka*), the heroic or inspiring (*virya*), the astonishing (*adbhuta*) and the peaceful (*santa*).

You are not artificial intelligence that remains without emotions and feelings. These nine states of emotional state are responsible for the fluctuations in mind. Sometimes you become as peaceful as Shiva; and sometimes you become as terrifying as demon. You exhibit a peculiar emotion at a time as per life situations. It defines your existence as a human. When the mind is at peace free from delusion, it does not long for anything nor does it reject anything.

Embracing this diversity of mind is essential, as it allows you to grow at 360 degree:

- Knowledge and understanding grow together
- Become aware of both (thought & feeling)
- Feel neither elated nor stressed
- Learn from others' strengths and weaknesses
- Appreciate the richness of human experience
- Cultivate empathy and understanding
- Celebrate individuality and creativity

Impact of Three Gunas on Mind

Krishna in *Bhagavad Gita* (3.28) declares that "The universe is maintained by the balance of opposing forces." World is dualistic in nature where opposition complement each other.

तत्त्ववित्तु महाबाहो गुण कर्म विभागयोः।
गुणागुणेषु वर्तन्तइतिमत्वान सज्जते।।

He who knows the truth that the Self is entirely distinct from the three Gunas and actions does not become attached to the actions. He who knows the truth about the classification of the Gunas and their respective functions understands that the alities as senseorgans move amidst the alities as senseobjects. Therefore he is not attached to the actions. He knows, I am Akarta - I am not the doer.

When dacoit *Angulimala* accepted Buddhism he said: "The past doesn't define the future." Everything is changing like the river. A sage becomes dacoit; and a dacoit becomes sage.

If you look at the unending space in dark night, you will notice moon, stars, planets, galaxy and a lot of beautiful brilliant lights. If you add-up together all that you can see, it will make up only five percent mass of the universe. And, astronomers and physicists have no idea of remaining 95 percent mass. In the same way, the whole humanity is familiar only with conscious mind.

Space is nothing but motley of dark and light. Light is associated with purity, harmony and balance (*sattva*); while dark is associated with ignorance, inertia and delusion (*tamas*). Both are contradictory; and interestingly complementary to each other. The glory of Ram in Ramayana is possible only because of misdeeds by Ravana, a character of action and passion (*rajo*).

You make decisions, make choices or react to situations depending on these three components that pervade the entire existence. An evil person uses his mind for only evil deeds, while a pure and pious person uses his mind to discover joy in everything without harming others. Mind is not a cut-and-dried formula which people can adopt and put into practice without training.

There are more than eight billion people in the world. There is absolutely no justification in the belief that man is a rational creature and his superiority over other creatures lies in his superior mind. But all minds, young and old, have a tendency to become attached. Some are attached to purity, love and contentment; while others are attached to impurity, hate and dissatisfaction.

भूमिरापोऽनलोवायुःखंमनोबुद्धिरेवच।
अहङ्कारइतीयंमेभिन्नाप्रकृतिरष्टधा।।भगवद्गीता, 7.4।।

Know that Prakrti, the material cause of this universe, which consists of endless varieties of objects and means of enjoyment and places of enjoyment, is divided into eightfold substances - earth, water, fire, air and ether, having smell, taste etc., as their attributes, and Manas along with kindred sense organs and the categories Mahat and ego-sense - all belonging to Me.

अपरेयमितस्त्वन्यांप्रकृतिंविद्धिमेपराम्।
जीवभूतांमहाबाहोययेदंधार्यतेजगत्।।भगवद्गीता, 7.5।।

This is My lower Prakrti. But know My higher Prakrti which is different from this, i.e., whose nature is different from this inanimate Prakrti constituting the objects of enjoyment to animate beings. It is 'higher', i.e., is more pre-eminent compared to the lower Prakrti which is constituted only of inanimate substances. This higher Nature of Mine is the individual self. Know this as My higher Prakrti through which the whole inanimate universe is sustained.

The five gross elements (*mahabhuta*) namely earth, water, fire, air and space are common among all people living in this earth. All are bestowed with the same organs of perception (*jnanendriyas*) and the organs of action (*karmendriya*). When the universal intelligence (*mahat*) manifests in individual, it breaks-down into *manas*, *citta*, *buddhi* and *ahamkara*.

Apart from the qualities of individual consciousness (*citta*), individual intelligence (*buddhi*) and ego (*ahamkara*), the individual mind (*manas*) fluctuates on the predominance of three basic components (*sattva, raja and tama*) that rules over the manifested existence. These three subtle basic elements are the very fabric of creation.

सत्त्वंरजस्तमइतिगुणाःप्रकृतिसंभवाः।
निबध्नन्तिमहाबाहोदेहेदेहिनमव्ययम्।।भगवद्गीता, 4.5।।

Sattva, Rajas and Tamas are the Gunas that arise from the Prakrti. They bind the immutable self in the body.

The *Bhagavad Gita* speaks of three primary qualities (*gunas*) which are present in different proportions in the whole nature including the human-beings. The permutations and combinations of these *gunas* and the predominance of one over the other are responsible for your behavior and internal disposition.

These three *gunas* are fluid and interchangeable. The main factors of changing mind are choices, associations and environment. So, one becomes deceived by one's own fickle mind. A person predominantly pure (*sattvic*) can become cruel (*tamasic*) due to circumstances or choices, while a lazy and ignorant one (*tamasic*) can shift towards action and passion (*rajasic*).

Thus, when *sattvaguna* is predominant, a person would behave in a soft and pure manner with love and compassion. When *rajoguna* is predominant, the same person would behave in a egoistic and self-centered manner with little concern for others. When *tamoguna* is predominant, the same person would behave in a lethargic and cruel manner.

Sattvic qualities: Wisdom, purity, clarity, optimism and inner joy.

Rajasic qualities: Anger, anxiety, fear, irritation, worry, restlessness, stress, action and courage

Tamsik qualities: Ignorance, fear, inertia, chaos and despair

Animals "*satvik*" in Nature

Satvik symbolizes purity, kindness, harmony and balance in life. Here are some animals/birds often associated with purity are:

- Cows--gentle, silent and contentment
- Deer--grace and innocence

- Rabbits--child-like simplicity and social in nature
- Dolphins--playfulness and harmony
- Swans---elegance and monogamous by nature
- Penguins--playful and pure

Rajas symbolize activity, passion, movement, desire, attachment and ego. Here are some animals/birds often associated with purity are:

- Lions--power, courage and regal
- Monkey--agility and mischievous
- Wild boars---strength and stubbornness
- Peacocks---pride and adoring
- Crows--intelligence and adaptability

Tamas symbolize darkness, inertia, confusion, ignorance and indolence. Here are some animals/birds often associated with purity are:

- Snakes--venomous, furious, active at night
- Crocodiles--cruel, short-tempered, aggressive
- Spider--dark, mystique, web of death
- Shark--ferocity and aggression
- Wolves---cruel, aggressive and deadly in nature

Intuitive Feelings and Opinions

The great fault of mind is that it doesn't know what to do with its information. Most of you don't know how to manage the mind. It has grown so dependent on false thinking and false beliefs that it makes you 'helpless' sometimes. Mind is conditioned shaped by limited perceptions, repetitive thoughts, dogmas and false beliefs.

You meet a stranger in a party or in busy market, and you instantly feeling comfortable or uneasy. Your mind gives subtle cues to navigate life. An intuitive mind knows without reasoning and understands without explanation. It sees patterns and connections and then makes instinctive decisions. Intuitive feelings are emotional intuition like sensing someone's mood.

Nobel Laureate Daniel Kahneman writes in his international bestseller *Thinking Fast and Slow* "The normal state of your mind is that you have intuitive feelings and opinions about almost everything that comes your way. You like or dislike people long before you know much about them; you trust or distrust strangers without knowing why......"

Individuals with distinct minds and orientation experience life distinctly, leading to varying opinions and feelings. A spiritual-oriented mind view life as interconnected and meaningful, and find joy in simplicity, nature and personal growth. While a materialistic bent of mind focus on pleasure, comfort and worldly success.

The mind's role is to witness and observe feelings, opinions and clouded judgment. Feelings and opinions seldom change. Some old memories (pleasing or unpleasing) keep bouncing in your sub-conscious mind and destabilize your mental state. Sometimes, you have to forget what's gone, appreciate what remains, and look forward to what's coming next.

Most of you might be familiar of the functioning of mind. In west, consciousness is considered to be faculty of mind; your consciousness exists in the mind. What east thinks about it? *Chitt* or universal consciousness becomes the mind by contraction. Mind is part of consciousness just like a river is part of the ocean. You could expand your mind, it would return to consciousness. Mind is like a bridge, of which one side is consciousness while on other side are sense organs. So we can say mind is the connecting fuse of consciousness and body.

Power of Mind

It is you who can speak to your mind. It's the mind that empowers you for observing your thoughts and emotions to evoke self-reflection and furthermore cultivate self-awareness and introspection. The mind has three levels--the lower mind (*manas*), the higher mind (*buddhi*) and the intuitive mind (*vijnana*). The lower mind is restless always oscillating from one thought to another. The higher mind encourages creativity and innovation.

Pablo Picasso and Leonardo Da Vinci used their higher mind that makes them immortal artists. Similarly, writers like Kalidasa, Tulsidasa, Premchand, William Shakespeare, and Thomas Hardy are examples who demonstrated the power of creative thinking, innovation and self-expression in fearless way. In the field of science, contributions of Newton, Einstein, Charles Darwin, J. C. Bose is great that exhibits their deep imagination, open-mindedness and critical thinking.

If you can understand it correctly and use it properly, it can bring transformation in your life. Although, mind has some limitations yet the seeker of Supreme can transcend its limitations and realize the highest truth. The mind is responsible for perception (*pratyaksha*), cognition (*jnana*), emotions (*bhava*), thoughts (*vritti*) and intellect (*buddhi*) as revealed in *Vedanta*.

You are able to communicate each other, understand each other because of the inherent power of mind. The power of mind is not easy to define. It covers a large variety of the activities of an individual in the personal, social and other spheres. Every phase of an individual's life is affected either favorably or unfavorably by what others do. Under these circumstances, it is necessary that the individual remains aware of what is happening around him.

"Man is the only creature that consumes without producing. He doesn't give milk, he doesn't lay eggs, he is too weak to pull the plough, and he cannot run fast enough to catch rabbits. Yet, he is lord of all animals", writes George Orwell writes in *Animal Farm*. Man's mind learns from various sources that makes him an edge over other creatures. He knows how gradually refined the mind that involves getting rid of depression, fear, anxiety and anger.

A spiritual mind is as powerful as creative mind of scientist or writer or poet. It is a intuitive mind of deeper understanding of real life that remains connected to Supreme Power to inculcate a sense of oneness and integrity. A divine mind has the ability to distance itself from pleasure, desire, success, money and other material gains of life. Lard Ram, Krishna, Buddha, Mahveer, Jesus, Adi Shankracharya, Guru nanak, Kabeer, Meera, Ramkrishna paramhamsh, Raman Mahrishi etc are some examples of spiritual minds all over the world.

If you don't know the instinctive power of your mind, you will have to rely on the mind of others. For a large portion, humans have no idea what they are talking about. Their mind travels faster than light. Wandering of mind is the greatest stumbling block in the way of spiritual progress. The problem is so old and gigantic that no cut-and-dried or speedy solution can be found. Your individual effort alone is not enough. You have to seek a awakened guru who can direct and instruct you in your divine pursuits.

Consciousness is One, Minds are Many

A passionate mind desires for love; and a dominating mind yearns for money, power etc. In fact, all craving is truly craving for only one thing: the fullness of divine consciousness. Consciousness is complete in itself, so there is no desire, crave or dream of anything. Wherever yours thought goes, mind takes its form. Mind is changing, so there are many divisions of mind. But the consciousness is unchanging, there is no further division.

It is binding energy of syllables (*matrika*) that makes it possible for you to understand words bind together as language. Language influences thought; and further thought influences mind. There are as many thoughts as waves on the surface of the ocean. Despite innumerable waves (thoughts), the ocean (consciousness) remains one, unchanged underpinning all minds. Consciousness means the reality of every mind.

Vijnanabhairava, Siva Sutras, Gita, Ramayana, Vedas and *Puranas* all scriptures agree unanimously that consciousness or reality or Brahman is one. It expresses itself in many minds like compassionate mind, contemplative mind, devotional mind, spiritual mind or ferocious mind, fearless mind, beast mind and the list is long. Devil and angel exists in every mind, as the manifested mind is dualistic. But the duality is only an appearance; it's not the ultimate truth.

Thinking is not possible without words. Mind means words, and words are sound. Birds and animals communicate through sounds, and every sound has specific meaning. See the *Bhagavad Gita*, chapter 7, verse 8-10, how beautifullyLord Krishna explain the manifestation of the divine in all things.

रसोऽहमप्सु कौन्तेय प्रभास्मि शशिसूर्ययोः।
प्रणवः सर्ववेदेषु शब्दःखेपौरुषंनृषु।।7.8।।

पुण्योगन्धः पृथिव्यांच तेजश्चास्मिविभावसौ।
जीवनं सर्वभूतेषु तपश्चास्मितपस्विषु।।7.9।।

बीजं मां सर्वभूतानां विद्धि पार्थ सनातनम्।
बुद्धिर्बुद्धिमतामस्मि तेजस्तेजस्विनामहम्।।7.10।।

बलं बलवतांचाहं कामराग विवर्जितम्।
धर्माविरुद्धो भूतेषु कामोऽस्मिभरतर्षभ।।7.11।।

I am the taste in the waters, O Arjuna! I am the light in the sun and the moon; the sacred syllable Om in all the Vedas; sound in the ether; and manhood in men am I. I am the pure smell in the earth; I am the brilliance in the fire; I am the life-principle in all beings, and austerity in ascetics. Know Me to be, the primeval seed of all beings. I am the intelligence of the discerning, and the brilliance of the brilliant. In the strong, I am strength, devoid of desire and passion. In all beings, I am the desire which is not forbidden by law (Dharma), O Arjuna.

Divine or supreme consciousness is present in every sound and every word. You may have fickle-mind (monkey mind) or fearless mind (lion mind) but all are fragment of cosmic mind. In the same way, *Vijnanabhairava* reveals that cosmic mind becomes embodied mind (*jiva*) by contraction when it manifests in individuals. Mind is part of cosmic mind just like all rivers are part of one ocean. And, it is your ignorance that sees divisions in forms and minds. Param Shiva (*Bhairava*) is that ultimate consciousness which destroys all ignorance. It happens only when all the fluctuations of mind come to end, and it becomes wave-less (*nistarang*).

A beautiful verse in *Ramcharitmanas*says that "Know that Ram is present everywhere in the universe (**सिया राम मय सब जग जानी, करहु प्रणाम जोरी जुगपानी**). Ravana is villainous character in *Ramayana*, but still his consciousness is as divine as any devotee of Lord Vishnu. In the divine play, it's the mind which sketches many characters but deep down, there is no differentiation between Ram and Ravan. It is the deepest non-dual understanding by Tulsidas to proclaim that Ram is all-pervading.

- Mind is mirror of every individual experience
- Knower is different from your mind
- What you experience is fragment of reality
- Mind can be managed or transformed
- Truth descends to him who see divinity in everyone

~~OM~~

Chapter 7

No-Mind State

Right now, you are not familiar with pure consciousness. Your consciousness is contaminated with the stuff of mixed mental-vital-physical components (*tattva*) out of which arises the movements of thought, emotion, sensation, impulse etc. The turbulent mind has to be silenced to allow grace descend to you. The mind stops and your hidden Buddha-nature shine forth.

Wherever your mind moves, your consciousness follows it. And, this is happening from many past lives. The forward-backward; upward-downward movement of mind creates multiple layers of ignorance, doubt and fear around the consciousness. In this process, the '*cit*' (pure consciousness) contracts and transforms into '*citta*' (contracted consciousness).

When mind becomes the master of your gross and subtle existence, you become devil. The cause of all human problems is erratic mind. When all thoughts cease, the existence is, and you are no more. No mind is a state of pure consciousness. Consciousness reflects on itself and on the divine dimension of its being. Before attaining no-mind state, learn of stilling the mind.

There is no 'self-remembering' in deep sleep. But in thought-free state, the outer world disappears, but the inner world remains alert. Thoughtlessness is a state of deep sleep in waking, a spontaneously thought-free state. Thoughtlessness state leaves your mind alone without thoughts of any forms and figures.

Children have no thoughts, but emotions. Their experiences are primarily driven by instincts, emotions, sensory perceptions and intuition. So, their thoughtless mind can't be equated to 'no mind' state. In no mind state, withdrawal (*laya*) of senses happens automatically leaving no space for emotion and perception. No mind state gives you immense '*ananda*' (bliss).

Direct Perception of Reality

The world you know is metaphysics and an attitude of mind. The pulsations of consciousness at deep sleep, certain moments of no-thought when there is very thin line between life and death--how shall you negate this no-mind state whose power and strength you feel? It is a pure conception without labeling or preconceptions. It is a state of no *vikalps* (mind-born concepts). It leads to direct perception of Reality as it is.

Transcending the limitations of mind is transformative to experience profound insights. Change is welcome, but not for its own sake. It is welcome, if it changes the world nearer to the heart's desire. To sustain your life, you need memory and imagination, but if you eager to explore subtle dimension of life, then mind is worthless. In no-mind state, you approach learning with a fresh, open perspective. And, it has no beginning and no end. It continues forever.

Whatever begins and ends is drama from Eastern philosophy's outlook. No matter, whatever you achieve and become in world, it remains a drama. So, if you become frightened, doubtful or worried of anything from any event, it's absurd. Even a thought of impending threat snatches all the peace and balance of your mind. Thought will not serve the purpose--be it thought of enlightenment or liberation. Whenever your mind is empty, divinity descends.

Think of your mind without any thoughts. Drop this thinking too, because thinking of no-thoughts is also a thought. Mind ceases automatically when it finds no support. In the absence of mind, senses become energy-less. When mind turns completely empty, you become the manifestation of void. This void within the void is known as no-mind state. When everything turns inwards, you become enlightened Buddha beyond all thoughts and imaginations.

Everything is energy or pulsations, so are your thoughts. Thought is like vibrations in the lake of your mind that no one can hear it except you. The sound of your thought has zero decibels. But still it has the capacity to carry your consciousness towards objective world. The non-stop inner chatting can distract you, disturb you and make you insane. Once you enter into inexpressible no-mind state, then you don't need any meditation or contemplation.

You will never know the 'unchanging' if you remain cling to changing. The changing world is only a fraction of the real. Whatever changes can't be original. You create your own world of misery by remaining attached to countless thoughts. Remain silent and crystal-clear like the water of a deep well to transcend mind (*manas*), intelligence (*buddhi*) and ego (*ahamkara*). No-mind state exclude the 'unreal' and merges with the real.

The mind is like a moving wheel where positive thoughts, negative thoughts and neutral thoughts rotate up and down. Your thoughtless state is your originality; when mind can't comprehend "I" (subject) and this or that (object). When objective consciousness and subjective consciousness finds nothing to cling on, you become the empty without desire, dream and ego. This is known as 'no-mind' in Zen Buddhism.

- No-mind is beyond duality (*dvaita*)
- Emotions and thoughts cease

- No influence of past experiences
- Dream-less state of mind
- You become the silent witness (*drishta*)

Frolicking Thoughts

A seed has no mind, no thoughts, no ego yet it grows into tree and gives fruits as a natural process. A river has no mind yet it flows effortlessly in the right direction without relying on Google map or man-made signboard. The mind is only a tool to help you navigating thoughts and make decisions. Your mind is not your true 'Self'.

Thought is merely a cloak which mind wears periodically and then replaces it with new thought (cloak) immediately. Thoughts remain engage in jumping, frolicking and hopping in the space of your mind. Like the kaleidoscope, mind changes the pattern of thoughts. So, during a 24 hour day, you become many in waking and dreaming state. Only in deep sleep, you become one.

There are many objects in this manifested world. As you can observe any one object, likewise you can observe what peculiar thought is moving in your mind at any time. No thought can live for more than few seconds, and it passes like sand between fingers. In your inner world, there is only one subject and you experience this reality only in 'no-mind' state.

That subject is all-pervading and there is no one in it but you. It remains hidden in the unbroken uproar of words. The deepest root of your existence comes in the surface only when the mind disappears in the profound stillness and peace found in the moments of solitude and quietness. You discover the subject as pure consciousness beyond thoughts and ego.

An empty mind or a mind with zero thoughts or the tide-less mind is known as no-mind state. You transcend the conditioned mind and there remains no identification with either ego or body. Shiva preaches *nistarang* (wave-less) aphorisms to Shakti in *Vijnanabhairava*. Thoughts collapse leads to emergence of pure consciousness state.

No thoughts or no mind is not a state. It is the reality on which thoughts appear. In meditation, you are able to observe the thoughts from the position of a no thought or no mind, which is the background on which thoughts appear. Cease being carried away by thoughts and naturally the concept of a thinker of thoughts will dissolve, leaving only the background on which thoughts appear and disappear.

You experience reality as it is because all barriers eliminates when thoughts drop in no-mind state. It has restorative effect on the consciousness. To experience 'no-mind', you have to rid one of thoughts or feelings or whatever tearing inside is. The first step is to remove craving from the mind. This process of negation expands your consciousness.

No-Mind State: Doorway to Divine

What is the true nature of divine? It is pure emptiness, pervades everything and this void is actually the ground of being. In fact, it is the foundation of self-inquiry urging individuals to let their consciousness pulsate purely to unearth the innate essence of their being. Divine is as transparent as cloudless sky, it's the mind that create illusions. No-mind state insists deep understanding of yourself wholly so that your mind doesn't fall into any illusion.

You don't struggle to breathe, it happens effortlessly. Breath is nearer to you, and most nearer to breath is 'divine' yet it is most difficult to perceive, for it is the power behind all perception via senses and mind. Divine is beyond space and time because it is not fixed in any one particular space or specific time. It is omnipresent-

-it is there wherever your mind goes and also wherever your mind doesn't go. No-mind state is between the two.

The fleeting nature of mind distorts your consciousness. Pure consciousness is beyond the duality of mind. If you bind your mind or if you free your mind, both are under your control. If mind is absorbed in *raga* (attachment) and *dvesha* (detachment); then it remains confined in the bondage of dualistic world. Attachment and detachment to thoughts create suffering. Let go of bondage and freedom to taste the bliss of divinity.

Mind is world and nothing else. It is filled with thoughts (positive, negative or neutral), experiences (pleasing or unpleasing), dreams (fulfilled or unfulfilled), time (past or future) and space (home or outside). What can be seen, observed or experience all are accumulated in the space of mind. To comprehend the world, you need mind. Divinity is nothing but pure consciousness fully conjoined with its innate power of insight.

The divine simplicity is not in kind and loving words but in the pure mind state bereft of any thoughts. Thoughts means disturbance. "The ultimate truth is indescribable," says Lao Tzu. It is beyond words and thought. You are divine by nature; it's your tearing thoughts that make all your experiences filtered. There is absolutely no problem; all problems are in the mind. No outer event can harm your true nature. Divine is your most intimate inner space.

No mind is quieting the mind. It happens on its own just like a flower blooms without intention. You need action (doing) to attain something ...accomplishments. But, Reality requires no effort, your being is enough. You need simple effortless awareness to transcend thoughts and conceptualization. Reality is direct unfiltered experience when all thoughts turn still in mind. This is the state of "*Turiya*" that *Advaita Vedanta* speaks about.

- Empty mind is supreme bliss
- There is no sense of "I"
- You dive into inner reality
- It is pathless path of stilling the mind
- Mind rests in the essential "Self"

No-Mind State: Useful in All Areas of Life

Mind and no-mind are poles apart. If you focus on the existing knowledge in your mind, you will continue to suffer. If you focus on the knowledge that you don't know, you will continue to grow. It's not an insurmountable task to release all thoughts without judgment. Pour out existing knowledge in your mind to make room for new. The greatest obstacle to learning new skill is your vagabond mind that resists anything new.

Does nothing just watch the content of your thoughts, and you will find that most are repetitive with new permutations and combinations. Thoughts are happening. You may have a elated feeling, be optimistic, have a sense of hope, or you may have a negative feeling. Thoughts come and go and can't stay forever in mind. Spiritual science is unearthing the mysteries of 'no-mind' state to truth-seekers every day. It is extending the bounds of human knowledge.

There is no virtue and no evil in mindfulness or thoughtless awareness. No-mind state is an esoteric state where thoughts, worries and distractions fade away, revealing your true nature. It requires a sensitive awareness and a feeling free from attachment and detachment to experience this state. It is a link between finite and infinite. To be in no-mind state even though for a moment, is to forget the 'fever and fret of this world'.

Inner silence is the hallmark of no-mind state. Silence is more important than chattering. You have to discard your entire mental and emotional realms of life. It is not necessarily the rejection or destruction of the past accumulated information; it is only an attempt to mould and modify the old patterns of thinking. Those who refuse to welcome changes are like the stinking waters of a stagnant pool. And stagnation means decay and death.

Usefulness:

- **Deeper concentration:** When the lake of the mind becomes crystal clear without any ripples, there remains no space for mental distraction. It helps in deeper concentration and thereby productivity soars.
- **Flexible mind:** Ordinary mind has tendency either to accept or reject anything that life or fate offers. Unshackled from thought patterns, no-mind state stirs your imagination and makes your mind flexible to adapt to changing environment.
- **Balancing state:** Conscious mind and unconscious mind are diabolical opposite. No-mind is neither tensed nor happy. He remains steady in happiness and distress. He handles the mind as a sailor handles a boat sailing in rough weather.
- **Makes you fearless:** Anxiety and worry dissolve in the calmness of no-mind. You roam in the world like a fearless lion.
- **Resist temptation:** It's effortless for a no-mind state to resist the temptation of shorter gains and continuing his graceful state without interruption. He wishes not to fulfill his own selfish needs but to do greater good of all concerned.

- **Creative relaxation:** No-mind enhances the feeling of relaxation, not a lethargic relaxation, but a creative relaxation that is intended to refine your whole being.
- **Deeper awareness:** The more you flow in awareness, the more joyous and easy is your experience of life. Creativity flows freely, undeterred by self-criticism
- **Personal growth:** The transformation is achieved through internalizing and minute observation. Self-awareness and introspection deepens.

Evolving through Silent Experiences

Any mind that abandons all thoughts, memories and experiences is fitting to enter the silence kingdom of divine. By nurturing 'no-mind' or silence state you transform the mechanical life and come closer to spiritual domain. Silence is the abode of spirituality. Silence is the sole master of mind. When mind struggles and surrenders to define the purpose of life in words, then silence quenches its thirst. There is Sufi proverb: "Silence is the language of gods".

In the book titled "The Myth of Sisyphus" Nobel Laureate author Albert Camus writes: "The mind's first step is to distinguish what is true from what is false. However, as soon as thought reflects on itself, what it first discovers is a contradiction". Every thought boomerangs in the mirror of your mind. The mind reflects its own thoughts. You may be poor, unfortunate, ugly and alone; still the mind is not ready to conceive this reality.

Thoughts are empty but your mind is not empty. Mind is keen to remember things without feeling bore. Thoughts are illusions so the mind is filled with non-sense stuff. Emptying the mind is pre-condition for Self-inquiry. Self is complete in itself and there is neither to add nor to delete. But, like an incorrigible child, mind is stubborn and seldom budges from its old habits. It goes on adding, no matter whether the information is useful or useless.

Your mind may think of yourself as 'special', but there is no specialty in any human. You exist as dust exists, flower exists, crow exists, and pebble exists. Sit in stillness whenever you get time surrounded by the fleeting nature of life and ponder over the simplicity of existence. All sentient and insentient things no matter how seemingly important or insignificant shares a common thread of impermanence. Everything returns to the earth ultimately.

Mind is outer world and no-mind is inner world. The outer is ever-changing, and the inner remains the same. One is impure; and the other is pure. Thinking is obstacle to the doorway of divine. When thoughts are tormented, you lose touch with the vital component of your being. To attain peace and bliss, you must learn to free your mind from all sorts of thoughts.

Your thoughts, emotions and experiences are all fleeting in nature; all subject to the whims of time. The boundaries of separation blur, and you recognize your existence as a part of whole in no-mind state. The king dies and the kingdom falls, but there is something within each individual that remains connected to the timeless essence. No-mind state is an attempt to grasp this reality through intuition, meditation and Self-inquiry.

- Feeling the 'unspeakable' untainted by thought
- Quiet mind stirs the inner awareness
- Hear the soundless sound of 'AUM'
- Eavesdrop on 'paravak' (celestial whisper)
- Unchanging reality is the essence of existence

Meditation vs. No-mind State

No-mind is a natural phenomenon. This no-mind state is the root of your origin. Whenever you seek happiness, joy and bliss inside, you attain zero-thought state. Multiplicity ceases, and only you shines in inner consciousness. No thought, no mind is needed, because you are a drop of infinite ocean of Ultimate bliss. Meditation seeks some support outside to turn the mind inside.

Bondage arises from some kind of 'thought' or 'emotion', either conscious or sub-conscious. Freedom is of two kinds, meditation and contemplation or reposing in no-mind state. The former is a training of the awareness of the mind; the latter is spontaneous state of thoughtlessness. Meditation is far more widespread and popular than no-mind state.

Mind draws the boundaries; no mind is complete freedom to let you in your own being. Meditation involves reducing inner talk and cultivates awareness of the present thought. Transcending world of thoughts through mind is herculean task. Mind's usual chatters disappear in moments of extreme crisis when you get trapped in life and death confrontations.

The purpose of meditation is to fight with your thoughts. No-mind state stress on let your mind is at ease. In the moment of sneeze, all thoughts disappear from the mind in a split of seconds and you attain no-mind state. When you eat something delicious, and become the taste where all thoughts vanish. These natural impulses must be transformed into complete freedom.

Awareness of thoughts is not enough. You can't be aware of your thoughts all the time except if you are awakened yogi. Unchecked thoughts often come into the mind giving rise to all sorts of evils. A man too conscious of thoughts becomes vain and aggressive. It generally leads to anger and hatred. Nobody questioned the need of 'no-mind' state in the past.

Meditation and 'no-mind' states are two most current terms in the spiritual science of modern world. They are often topics of controversy. And spiritual thinkers and practitioners try to strike a balance between the two. Meditation is stepping-stone to a thoughtless state that is characterized by tranquil mind--free from duality, separation and conditioned responses.

Vital energy (*prana-shakti*) is the driving force behind the emergence of all thoughts and emotions. A mind consumed by all forms of thoughts finds no relief in the world. In the stillness of mind, the flow of thoughts stops on its own. No-mind state can certainly be seen as a form of meditation. A state without duality leaves no footprints in your consciousness.

The primary function of a meditation, as the very name suggest, is to withdrawal of mind and senses to inward. Common practice of meditation often involves breath-awareness, mantra recitation, or focusing on any specific object. No-mind state can arise spontaneously without meditation. Thought processes stop in deep sleep due to disconnection from external stimuli.

- Meditation is relaxing rejuvenation of mind & body
- No-mind state is effortless shift in thoughtlessness
- Meditation can lead to no-mind state
- No-mind can separate the body from suffering
- You see yourself in thoughtless state

Simple Tips to Still the Mind

Mind has an obstinate tendency to get easily lost in slight distractions. You see a beautiful house while roaming in nearby street. And, mind instantly dreaming of owning that house. You sit in some sort of meditation, and suddenly flashback memories start emerging and all your effort to still the mind go in vain. Mind drags you forcibly to the familiar world.

Mind is 'devil' that can take any form. Like clouds, thoughts float into the mind's vast sky, morphing into diverse shapes and sizes. Some are bright and appeasing signaling hope and sunshine. Others loom dark and dreary, unleashing storms of anxiety and fear. These mental clouds can snatch peace and freedom, casting shadows on the mind's serenity.

You can't be aware of every thought that appears in some corner of your mind. You remain agitated by mental upheavals. So, the noble thought of emptying the mind remains elusive. However, traditional techniques of simple meditation are imperative for novice who is eager to taste the thoughtlessness state of mind.

The simplest way to still the mind is breath-meditation. Breath is spontaneous, so it's easy to fix the mind on the incoming and outgoing movement of breath. When your awareness and the breath unites and becomes one, mind stops wandering. Outer world disappears in serene, calm and still mind. Buddha attained enlightenment by practicing breath-awareness.

Most of the people are fickle-minded. Mind is restless by nature. Senses are intoxicated and seek pleasures and gratification most of the time. It's not a child play to quiet the turbulent mind. "Closing all the doors of the senses and fixing the mind on the heart and the life air at the top of the head, one establishes himself in yoga" (*Bhagavad Gita*, chapter 8, verse 12).

सर्वद्वाराणि संयम्य मनोहृदिनिरुध्यच।
मूर्ध्न्याधायात्मनः प्राणमास्थितो योगधारणाम्। ।8.12। ।

If you become proficient in breath-awareness, then one day you will also be aware of that point where breath stops for split of seconds. The retention of breath (*kumbaka*) happens on its own at inner space and outer space where inhale ends and exhale ends simultaneously. When breath stops mind also becomes empty although momentarily.

You may be walking, thinking, talking or doing some task, your awareness must be inclusive in the gap between incoming and outgoing breath. This is one of the traditional meditation techniques which Shiva reveals to Shakti in *Vijnanabhairava*. This is the natural way of stilling the mind and grab hold of your fickle mind.

When breath awareness deepens in day-to-day life, like the cloudless sky, the mind remains unchanged, witnessing thoughts pass by. As clouds dissipate, mental clarity emerges, revealing the mind's innate calmness. By acknowledging thoughts without judgment, one can reclaim his inner peace and serenity.

Here are some simple tips to tame the mind:

- Practicing traditional meditation techniques to quite the mind
- Mantra meditation bring your mind to the present moment
- Immerse yourself into the wisdom thoughts of *Bhagavad Gita* (or other epics)
- Indulge in simple walking meditation to withdraw senses
- Empty your mind while listening to the sound of ever-flowing river
- Feel the consciousness of others as your own one

From Where Thoughts Come and Go

No-mind state is not a state of nothingness, but an overflowing state of bliss, freedom and consciousness. It is a state of completeness which is the supreme source of all gross, subtle and subtlest existence. Thoughts belong to subtle state; while no-mind belongs to your subtlest existence source of all your thoughts, emotions and reactions to senses impulse.

No mind is solitary state where your limited consciousness merges with the Self. In the screen of mind thoughts emerge, move and disappear, and no-mind is the projector which throws light on the screen. In the depth of your existence lies a profound mystery: where you only exists as no-mind consciousness or pure consciousness.

In ordinary talk, you need two people—one speaks and other listens. In inner chatting, only your mind is needed. In both cases, thoughts are basic foundation. All thoughts arise from the void state (no-mind), taking shape as ephemeral mental matrix. Like waves on the ocean's surface, thoughts swell, crest, and dissipate, finally returning to the unfathomable depths.

Swelling of waves loses itself in cresting; cresting of waves loses itself in dissipation. Waves come and go but ocean remains undisturbed and unchanged. This eternal cycle underscores the impermanence of thought and the boundless potential of the void. In a simple and beautiful analogy, "If no-mind state is the ocean, then thoughts are a wave."

Mind can be many; but no-mind is one. You may have divine thoughts; or you may have dirty thoughts depending which state (*sattva, rajasic* or *tamasic*) is dominant. In no-mind state, you transcend all three states of nature (or *maya*). Any one state is limited and cannot exist without the other two, but the no-mind state can, for it is the inexpressible ground of all three.

Mind may stay in the no-mind, but world shouldn't stay in the mind. Existence of world in your mind makes a wall between you and your essential existence. This paradoxical concept challenges your conventional understanding, as you typically equate world with something--pleasing or unpleasing. However, the no-mind state reveals that void is:

- The source: The wellspring from which thoughts emerge
- The sink: The abyss into which thoughts dissolve
- The substratum: The underlying reality supporting the flux of thought

Characteristics of the no-mind state

- Thoughts cease and the mind becomes still
- Awareness transcends thought
- Past and future converge into present
- Inner silence carry you to liberation

To experience this profound state of no-mind:

- Feel the tranquility of zero thoughts
- Sharpens awareness of the present moment
- Go beyond attachment and detachment
- Don't get trapped in illusive world (*maya*)

By acknowledging the no-mind state:

- Attain absolute spiritual freedom
- Your inner world is drenched in love
- Everything seems to be perfect and fine
- Relate every being to positive dimension

--OM--

Chapter 8

Psychology of Mind

A lot of people don't care about knowing the working of mind because they don't speculate the adverse effect of reckless mind. It is important to convince people to care about the desires, dreams, attachments and aversions filled in their multiple layers of thoughts. The purpose of understanding the psychology of mind is to cleanse your souls from the dust that mind accumulates of everyday life. Turn your mind in soul-searching in spite of aimless wandering.

Mind is vulnerable to many enticements of life--be it money, love, praise, recognition etc. It makes you anxious, excited and never at piece and the whole life is wasted in wild-goose chase. It fills you with negativity and you see the same wherever you go. The psychology of mind knows what your mind thinks, feel and behave in changing environment. Mind has primarily three functions think and emotions and makes strategy to cope with challenges.

It aims to:

- Understand human behavior
- Improve mental health
- Enhance human interaction

- Promote empathy
- Foster individual growth

Science of Human Behavior

The scientific study of mental processes, emotions and thoughts has taken long strides during the last century. In a breakthrough discovery in "neuro-technology" reveals that brain-computer interfaces have enabled users to control devices with their thoughts. These discoveries are updating our understanding of the mind. Science advances so fast that it is really not possible to predict what further miraculous developments will be made in the near future.

The psychology of mind is study human behavior in a joint collaboration of neuroscience, sociology and traditional Indian philosophy. The neuroscience deals with understanding brain function and role of neurons in transmitting messages to other organs of the body. Sociology examines cultural influences on the individual behavior. While quieting of mind by meditation and self-inquiry are the foundations of traditional philosophy that delves deeper into mind.

The psychology of mind is amazing, but it is questionable, if mind is blessing or a curse, a devil or an angel. So far its blessings have been mixed--in fact more devilish than angelic. For every one problem that it has solved, it has created a dozen new problems. Neuropsychologists, cognitive psychologists, clinical psychologists, social psychologists and positive psychologists speculate over the miraculous possibilities of the working of mind.

Here are some striking features of the mind:

- Mind is vulnerable to cognitive illusion
- You see what you have in your heart
- The calmer you are, better clarity of thoughts

- Awareness refines your experiences

Tremendous Convincing Power of Mind

Feelings, thoughts, beliefs and actions give birth to greed, desires and fears and these are basic challenges to human existence. Ordinary mind seeks material success, and leaves no stone unturned to realize its dreams and desires. But, somehow, if not successful, it takes U-turn. No one choose to become spiritual, it just circumstances happened and you attract towards spirituality. It's not your intuition, but egoistic mind that instructs you to change the path.

In a thought-provoking "*doha*" (couplet), Kabir says:

तन को जोगी सब करे, मन को करे ना कोई।
सहजे सब सिद्धि पाइए, जो मन जोगी होय।।

Spiritual practitioners only dyed their robes and not their hearts. If they do so, all occult powers will be gained naturally.

Spirituality is not an escapist path to feed your defeated ego and desires. As long as there is "I", there is no possibility of spiritual evolution no matter what you wear, pray or read scriptures. Accepting life without judging it or resisting it is the ultimate thing in this less-travelled path.

Money and power are two core values of this fleeting world. Uncontrolled mind is vulnerable to greed of accumulating more and more and at the same time, fear of losing what is in your possession. To a conditioned mind, the charm of world is irresistible. Mind wants everything that you think it will make you happy. Don't trust your monkey mind. Instead, hear what the inner guide is desperate to instruct you in a situation when you are failure in your mission.

Mind is the cause of any success or failure in the world. The human mind in absence of wisdom possesses an unparalleled ability to rationalize, justify and convince. This convincing power can be both a blessing and a curse, influencing your thoughts, emotions, and actions. The mind's adaptability and resilience enable it to explore life's complexities, but also lead to self-deception and destructive tendencies.

There is a growing trend of seeking spirituality in western world. The uncertainty of life instills fear in mind. When faced with material failure or disappointment, the mind may shift towards spirituality, seeking solace and meaning. This transformation can be genuine, leading to personal growth and self-awareness. However, it can also serve as an escape from worldly responsibilities, allowing individuals to justify their failures as 'fate' or '*karma*'.

The problems of material existence can't be solved by accumulation of wealth. When you commit sins just for materialistic gain, the mind employs clever rationalizations to justify your behavior. The concept of "*tamasic*" traits in Hindu philosophy--characterized by darkness, ignorance and chaos--can be misused to excuse your wrongdoings. The mind convinces you that your actions are inevitable or necessary, given the circumstances.

Conversely, when you achieve success, the mind can fuel your ego, breeding greed and selfishness. Your accomplishments become proof of your superiority, and you start believing that you deserve more. The mind rationalizes your desires, convincing you that your actions are justified by your accomplishments.

Bhagavad Gita very beautifully said-

प्रकृतेः क्रियमाणानि गुणैः कर्माणि सर्वशः।
अहङ्कारविमूढात्मा कर्ताऽहमिति मन्यते।।3.27।।

It is the Gunas of Prakrti like Sattva, Rajas etc., that perform all the activities appropriate to them. But the man, whose nature is deluded by his Ahankara, thinks, 'I am the doer of all these actions.' Ahankara is the mistaken conception of 'I' applied to the workings of Prakrti which is not the 'I'. The meaning is that it is because of this (Ahankara), that one who is ignorant of the real nature of the self, thinks, 'I am the doer' with regard to the activities that are really being done by the Gunas of Prakrti.

Spirituality leads to unity; materialism to diversity. The fundamental role of mind is in shaping your identity, perceptions and manifested reality. The convincing power of mind reveals the mind's duality in enabling you to cope with adversity and leading you astray with rationalizations. It has far-reaching consequences:

- Spiritual bypassing: Avoiding personal growth through superficial spirituality
- Moral disengagements: Justifying your own self-destructive actions
- Egotistical entrapment: Becoming prisoners of your own success.

(East and West must establish a golden middle path of activity and spirituality combined, he continued. India has much to learn from the West in material development; in return, India can teach the universal methods by which the West will be able to base its religious beliefs on the unshakable foundations of yogic science)

(Babaji's Interest in the West, *Autobiography of a Yogi* by Paramahansa Yogananda)

Inner Conflict

What you speak, feel and react is the outcome of the forces of mind. Recognizing the mind's dual nature is the first step before analyzing the psychological mechanism. Spiritual specialists and psychologists know that mind in itself is useless. It needs some support--it can be of thought, idea, belief, memories or instinct--to let it allow in flowing state. There always come a moment when one must choose between conditioned mind and the pure mind.

The feeling of inner conflict is at first only a suggestion by mind; it becomes a reality once your embodied consciousness accepts it. It is like a wrong advice in the mind; if the mind accepts it, it goes deep into the sub-conscious part of mind. You become confused what to accept and what to reject while taking any critical decision. If your inner voice suggest you to drop any idea; you must not accept the mind but reject it with whole consciousness.

All thoughts, ideas or feelings pass through vital-physical sheath of the subtle consciousness and subtle body before they manifest. Mind can do nothing and yet it can do everything. An attached and egoistic mind can indeed create suffering, while a controlled mind can lead to insightful transformation. When you start flowing in the outer world and forget your subjective consciousness, it gives you mental anguish and emotional turmoil and misguided perceptions.

The mind's tendency to think highly of individual one while finding fault in others is a fundamental aspect of human nature. This dichotomy leads to inner conflict, influencing your relationship, self-perception and overall well-being. This mindset leads to inner conflict where individual struggle with self-doubt and criticism.

Mind is a battleground of conflicting thoughts. This mind and this world wrestle against each other without being able to embrace each other. Self-deception is a pervasive and intriguing phenomenon where individuals unconsciously distort or deny reality to avoid uncomfortable truths. This paradoxical process entraps you in your own deception, leading to a distorted perception of yourself and the world.

You may be rich, successful and respected in society, but you can't deny the inner conflict of mind. Either you can be conscious of the external surroundings, or you can be conscious of the inner happenings in your mind. Usually, your attention is on outer projections of the mind. Mindfulness attempts to rises above the outer environment and directs your awareness to the inner world. It helps to make the mind tranquil and calm like the wave-less water of a lake.

You are not perfect, although everyone thinks he is perfect. Everyone is just like everyone else. No one is free from inner conflicts that arise from the complex interplay between various psychological, emotional and social factors. Here are some causes:

Psychological factors: Whatsoever happens you remain dissatisfied owing to dualistic nature of mind, inconsistent thoughts, prejudices and assumptions, fear & anxiety and worries related to future.

Emotionalfactors: The dust gathers in mind due to emotional turmoil, strained relationships, negative self-talk (inner chattering), unfulfilled desires and suppressed emotions.

Social factors: You never feel blissful due to dogmatic cultural family, communication gap, multiple responsibilities, conflicting obligations and non-accepting mind.

Adopting a Winning Mindset

This mindset is a subject of psychologists, educationists and policy-makers who use the scientific method to study the mind, including how it relates to perceptions, behavior and brain functioning of a performer. This is a big world of winners or losers who share the same space and you are also one of them. The modern science has presented comforts, luxuries and conveniences to all its inhabitants, but its impact on your mindset is constrained.

Obstacles are harsh realities of life. But a determined person never surrenders instead overcome obstacles by learning valuable lessons from failures. J.K. Rowling's best-seller book "Harry Potter" was rejected dozen times by many publishers, but she remained in her balanced state of mind. Never say die spirit is a time-tested path to winners. It means never giving up, even when things seem impossible. This mindset can turn you into a winner.

There is no such as an overnight success. People have always marveled at the irksome way in Dashrath Manjhi who single-handedly carved a path through a mountain in Bihar. He displayed a great deal of persistent hard work of 22 years which was amazing. This stupendous success did not come easily to him. Years of dedication and disciplined training went into making his success possible. People noticed his victory, but not his struggle.

Hockey stalwart Major Dhyan Chand was born in a very poor family in the Colonial India. He had not enough money to purchase hockey stick, and he used to practice dribbling ball with an umbrella. His skill impressed the German's dictator Adolf Hitler in Berlin Olympics. His flawless ball control, quick reflexes and a unique ability to score goals in challenging situation is written in golden letters in the history of Indian sports.

Do you know what makes you winner? There may be many factors, like hard work, dedication, persistent, but the foremost is self-confidence. A winner doesn't doubt his/her ability, no matter, what others say. No one becomes winner at the first attempt. You may be loser in may attempts, but remember, every setback is a chance for an applauded comeback. You become what you think. Positive thoughts always lead to winning a medal.

"The vision of a champion is someone who is bent over, drenched in sweat, at the point of exhaustion when no one else is watching."

Jim Afremow,

The Champion's Mind

Jim is a world renowned sports psychologists who has helped dozens of athletes prepare for the Olympic Games. You need to think like a champion--be it at work or in sports. Prepare beyond your goals and execute like your life depends on it. One major reason for failure is low self-esteem, doubt, prejudice and selfishness. The solution lies in a balanced integration of thoughts, emotions and executions to grow internally and bring success in your chosen field.

There is a common factor in the lives of all great achievers they exercised their desire, dream and vision in small ways that made great impact on their lives and left indelible footprint in the mind of success-seekers. By understanding this winning mindset, you can move forward, with confidence, in the direction of your dreams. And, last but not the least, do your best and leave rest to divine will. Remember, God helps those who helps themselves.

Here are some inputs to inspire yourself to do the impossible:

- Face all hindrances bravely and keep going on
- Overcome fears, doubts and anxieties
- Keep target in mind and don't swings between dos and don'ts
- Nurture winning habits and give-up defeating mindset
- Accomplish most difficult tasks by resilience
- Reach your maximum potential

Spiritual Manipulation: Art of Psychology

In this age of money and materialism, who cares for spiritual growth and transformation? Spiritualism has become a business, and like a true businessman, so-called spiritual gurus use every application and tools to woo listeners and entice them to become their followers. They firmly believe in "*jo dikta hai vo bikta hai*" (what appeals to the eyes, sells). They know that their audience plus followers are their lifeblood of their business.

The problem of helpless persons is rampant in India. Today, it has assumed wide dimensions. In every nook and corner of India, one can see desperate crowd of unemployed skilful youth, poor farmers with no land, estranged wife, son/daughter of separated parents running after the religious gurus to seek solace and peace. They want escapism from harsh realities of life. They seek advice and sermon from spiritual scholars to ensure transformation in life.

Gullible are easily exploited who easily believe whatever other speaks or instruct them to do so. Spiritual speakers and motivational speakers often tap into this common psychological mindset like believing in fate, religious sentiments and mental conditioning of considering world as an illusion. Many spiritual gurus present teachings that reverberate well with common parlance, but true enlightenment is often a deeply personal and subjective experience.

More than reality, people's imagination is horrible. They don't have patience to wait for silver lining in the moment of darkest cloud. In uncertain times, people often turn to spiritual guidance for divine support and hope. Spiritual gurus can provide a sense of stability helping followers navigate their fears about the future. They identify the specific subject or topic the followers are passionate about and where they can offer the most value.

Spiritual orators and motivational speakers exploit human vulnerabilities, preying on fear, doubt and desperation. The content of their speech (of spiritual gurus & motivational speakers) mainly focus on the psychology of mind--they are able to address people's inner world, which in turn influences behavior and emotional well-being. It's enchanting how they connect psychology with spirituality to make their teachings impactful.

In reputed English-daily "Financial Express" (dated March 20, 2024) report titled "Seven richest spiritual gurus in India" speaks of the enormous wealth they accumulated:

- Sadhguru Jaggi Vasudev: Rs 200 crore (estimated net worth)
- Asaram Bapu: Rs 350 crore (estimated net worth)
- Sri Sri Ravi Shankar: Rs 1000 crore (estimated net worth)
- Gurmeet Ram Rahim Singh: Rs 1455 crore (estimated net worth)
- Mata Amritanandamayi (Amma): Rs 1500 crore (estimated net worth)
- Baba Ramdev: Rs 1600 crore (estimated net worth)
- Sadhguru Nithyananda: Rs 10,000 crore (estimated net worth)

Finally, when some conman see the trade of spiritual leaders and motivational speakers flourishing and established persons in respective fields are becoming wealthy every year, they enter the profession with half-baked knowledge. We must safeguard our society against them. They exploit human vulnerabilities, preying on fear, doubt and desperation. They cleverly manipulate psychological weaknesses, masquerading as enlightened ones:

- *Hopelessness:* Religion acts as opium for hopeless persons. Conman know this fact very well, and they extract money in the name of divine blessings.
- *Playing on fear:* Creating anxiety about spiritual consequences or promised salvation
- *Exploiting doubt:* Offer false certainty that everything will be fine in the end

- *Exclusive treatment:* Offering rare knowledge to selected followers or disciples
- *Quick solutions*: Promising quick fixes, exploiting desperation for solutions

Why Mind Oscillates between Extremes?

Worldly mind roam here and there on the wheels of lust, greed, anger, envy, deceit, attachment and pride. When it gets bore, the same mind begins seeking salvation via meditation, prayer, chanting, pilgrimage and intense penance (*sadhana*). Object may change, but the egoistic mind remains the same. The world never disappears in both states of mind. Until one attains true wisdom, all the fluctuations of mind are psychological. In *Bhagavad Gita,* Arjuna asked some question regarding the nature of mind to Lord Krishna.

चञ्चलं हि मनः कृष्ण प्रमाथि बलवद्दृढम्।
तस्याहं निग्रहं मन्ये वायोरिव सुदुष्करम्।।6.34।।

Arjuna asked O Krsna ! The mind is indeed unsteady, destructive, strong and obstinate; to control it, I believe, is very difficult, just as to control the wind.

For the mind, which is found to be fickle even in matters incessantly practiced, cannot be firmly fixed by a person in one place. It agitates that person violently and flies away stubbornly elsewhere. Regarding such a mind, which by nature is fickle even in matters practiced, I regard that its restraint and fixing in the self, which is of ite opposite nature, is as difficult as restraining a strong contrary gale with such things as a fragile fan etc. The meaning is that the means for the restraint of the mind should be explained.

श्रीभगवानुवाच:

असंशयं महाबाहो मनो दुर्निग्रहं चलं।
अभ्यासेन तु कौन्तेय वैराग्येण च गृह्यते। ।6.35। ।

The lord Krishna said O mighty-armed! No doubt, the mind is unsteady and is hard to control. But it is controlled by practice and through an attitude of desirelessness.

No doubt, the mind is hard to subdue on account of its fickle nature. However, it can be subdued with difficulty by cultivating favorable attitude in the direction of the self by repeated contemplation of Its being a mind of auspicious attributes (these being eternality, self-luminosity, bliss, freedom from Karma, purity etc.), and by the absence of hankering produced by seeing the host of evil alities in objects other than the self hankered for.

Inconsistency of thoughts is the major cause of dissatisfaction. Psychology says that many evil people who gather enormous wealth by unfair means thinks that visiting holy shrine and then donating some money to poor ones will neutralizes their misdeeds. An unethical person can't be spiritual just by generating noble thoughts or donating something to needy. The great philosopher Epictetus rightly said: "You cannot hope to make progress in areas where you have taken no action."

Mind oscillates like a pendulum because it needs stimulation. If you are not doing new things, or learning new skills, mind gets stuck like the water of seasonal rivulet. Even hearing the same news again and again, the mind finds it intensively boring. Repeating the same dreary work with no enthusiasm is no longer satisfying, interesting or stirring in any way. If you are passionate about your work, then the same repetitive work can be rejuvenating.

Mind is merely an instrument to experience 'life' through cognitive senses. But the problem arises when one identifies himself/herself with mind or body or combo of both. The same carefree mind in calm state doesn't take interest in spiritual domain of life is seen shifting towards divinity at the time of storm. If you think of this world merely as a monotonous and boring, think again. You can discover liveliness in performing the mundane.

Human mind is neither fully conscious nor fully unconscious, but partly both. Indeed, within every person lies the potential for both--moving towards fully conscious (divine) or towards fully unconscious (demon). It all depends on which state your emotions are churning (*satvic, rajasic* and *tamasic*). The physical nature is constantly changing (**अधिभूतं क्षरो भावः**:*Gita*, chapter 8, verse 4), so is your mind. Your mind is influenced by both inner and outer factors.

The ordinary mind is fickle by nature; it can't stick to one specific point. What draws the mind towards spirituality and what motivates the mind to chase the material world? Mahatma Gandhi was mesmerized with western culture when he was a law student in London. But when he returned India in 1915 and visited many villages in remote areas, he shifted towards simple living, wearing minimal clothes and eating food just to sustain life.

The famous Beatles group visited India in late 1960s, and their chance meeting with Maharishi Mahesh Yogi changed their lifestyle. That musical concert group that was known for lavish lifestyle started meditation in Rishikesh. In fact, they were so fed-up with glitter world of wine and women that their mind was looking for escapism. But it all turned out to be nine days wonder. Soon, their mind started looking for glamorous world of modernity.

The human mind is a restless entity, constantly seeking new experiences and stimulation. It is programmed to explore, question and evolve, leading to perpetual cycle of desire and dissatisfaction. In material pursuits, the mind initially finds comfort in the tangible—wealth, status and physical pleasures. However, as these external achievements accumulate, they often fail to provide lasting contentment.

The fleeting nature of material success leaves a void, prompting the mind to shift its gaze towards spirituality, hoping to fill that inner emptiness with meaning, purpose, and connection to something greater than itself. Yet, paradoxically, those deeply entrenched in spiritual life can experience their own form of dissatisfaction. A life devoted solely to the pursuit of spiritual enlightenment can sometimes feel detached from the pleasures and joys of physical existence.

The ascetic life, with its demands of renunciation and discipline, may create a longing for the richness and vibrancy of the material world. Thus, the spiritual seekers may find themselves yearning for the experiences they once left behind—earthly pleasures, human bonding, and the simple joys of living. This constant back-and-forth reflects the duality within human nature.

On one hand, we are driven by the desire for material success and enjoyment, while on the other; we seek deeper meaning, peace and transcendence. The mind, albeit fickle, is rarely content with one state for too long. It craves balance but often oscillates between extremes. The balance of the mind, self-control and awareness are what can lead a person to their innate true nature of consciousness.

Overcoming Old Habits and *Samskaras* (Impressions)

Nowadays, thoughts and mental impressions stored in human's psyche do not find a place in the modern lifestyle. Many people postpone their working on mental grooves thinking that they will do it tomorrow. But tomorrow never comes. All stress is laid on career, money and status in society. This results into the formation of split personalities.

Unlike machines, every human have feelings, emotions and dreams. Trying to make your dreams come true is natural instinct. Most of you like others failed at something so miserably that they surrender to the fate and never try again. But positive psychology says that your grit lies not in falling, but in rising every time you fail.

Old *samskaras* (mental impressions) can have a deep impact on your behavior, thoughts and emotions. These impressions accumulate over time based on your experiences, habits and reactions, sometimes creating negative mental patterns. You are all meant to grow and stretch despite challenging circumstances and your limitations.

Failing teaches you how to be perseverant and keep going for your dreams. Each failure makes you understand what to do and what not. Doing well, in any activity, for example, a sport, music, dance, painting or learning any new language, involves a great deal of struggle. Most of you might be nervous to begin with until gradually you overcome fears and perform well.

Grit can be developed by not accepting defeat. Instead, you should make efforts whole-heartedly to overcome your limitations, and not stay down. One of the techniques that help is meditation that stills the puzzling mind and focus on the present moment. When you discover pleasure in your work, the mind releases endorphins that shift your mood and you begin to look at the brighter side.

To bring positively to your mind's psychology and dissolve old *samskaras*, one can follow these steps:

- Self-observation: Pay attention to your thoughts, emotions and reactions. Identify recurring negative patterns and *samskaras*. This is the first step to transformation.

- Mindfulness meditation: Practicing mindfulness helps you observe your thoughts without attachment or judgment, gradually dissolving their power over you.
- Breath-awareness: Controlled breathing awareness removes energetic blocks and helps to release deep-rooted *samskaras*.
- Cultivate positive habits: Regularly practice gratitude, compassion and kindness to create new, positive *samskaras*
- Letting go of attachment: *Samskaras*often persist because of emotional attachment to past events (good or bad). Practicing work without attachment helps to release these suppressed emotions and tearing thoughts.
- Chanting mantra recitation: Chanting sacred mantras like *aum*, *soham* etc. can have a purifying effect on the mind. It helps cleanse the mind of deep-rooted impressions, leading to greater mental clarity and positivity.
- Detoxifying mind and body: Few thing, are more dreadful than weak body and disturbed mind. Walking or strolling in the sylvan surroundings of nature helps in detoxification of mind and body. It helps the individuals to stop the self-sabotaging downward spiral of hopelessness, despair and frustration.

~OM~

Chapter 9

Evolution of Mind

If the forefathers of earlier civilizations could somehow were to visit this world now, they would indeed be wonderstruck by the incredible advancements in technology and society. Airplanes, submarines, and skyscrapers would seem mystic or supernatural to them, given that their understanding of the world was shaped by more basic tools and natural phenomena. They might marvel at our accomplishments and struggle to understand how we arrived here.

Animals (including other creatures) have remained largely the same, but humans have transformed their life to an almost "superhuman" level. The human mind's capacity for innovation and creativity has allowed us to push the limitations of what's possible. We have taken control over many aspects of life that were once out of reach. The "super mind" is indeed at the heart of human advancement and is sure to bring about more wonders in future.

Incredible Journey

In physical strength, man is no match to lion and gorilla. Tortoise and elephant lives longer than any man. Cheetah runs faster than 100 m gold medalist in Olympics. It's the evolution of human mind that makes him superior to other creatures. From hunting to farming; from bullock-cart to space voyage; in these entire million years journey; the superiority of human is unquestionable. The human mind has grown vertically and horizontally (*in terms of functioning*).

The brain function of Homo sapiens was simple--it remained focused on food gathering, sleeping, procreation and safety from predators and nature's calamity. The human brain has remained same for 200,000 years, but the average size of the brain relative to the physical composition has decreased by three to four percent in the last 100 centuries. The brain has now become more complex with extra cortical areas and the separation of the neo-cortex.

And the most interesting is that mind's basic reason-ability, problem-solving aptitude; inner and outer understanding including wisdom has grown exponentially. And, the major credit goes to introduction of culture segregation, religious impact and education system at early age changed the way that expanded mind's ability to innovate and create new things. The evolution of mind has also been shaped by biological, environmental and social pressures.

No part of the human history remained free from challenges. The story of the evolution of the brain is story of nervous system. Even *Charak Samhita* describes brain as a seat of vital energy (*prana*) and sensory faculties. Brain needed for coordinating and governing the various parts of the body. Social brain hypothesis suggests that the human brain evolved in response to the complexities of livings in social groups.

Neolithic age was a transformative one in human's history that heralded farming nearly 12,000 years ago. The knowledge of farming was passed down across generations. The evolution of the mind refers to expressions of emotions and feelings in most refine way; crystal clear thinking and understanding capacity; groundbreaking scientific discoveries and inventions; and most interestingly, human mind is still evolving.

The upright posture and bipedal movement re-define the sensory and motor functions of the brain. Earlier, the sensory function of our organs in coordination with the hands and legs movement was not sharp. It paved the way for the rise of vertebrates (brain expansion). Once humans began walking on two legs, it not only freed up their hands for using tools but also seemed to kick-start the development of a more complex brain.

Human evolution is the long and complex process by which modern humans (Homo sapiens) developed from their ancestors over millions of years. The tale of human evolution begins some seven million years ago, with the emergence of the first human-like ancestors. These species have small brains and showed the earliest signs of bipedalism (ability to walk on two legs).

The evolution of mind refers to the development of cognitive practices in human. This process is closely linked to biological evolution, where natural selection favored traits that improved survival and reproduction. Early *Homo sapiens* had roughly the same brain size as modern humans, around 1,200 to 1,500 cm^{3}. Early humans had less specialized brains compared to different patterns of cortical folding and neural connectivity.

Early homo sapiens demonstrated basic cognitive abilities, such as tool use, simple communication, and some level of abstract thinking, as evidenced by early art and burials. These capacities were critical for survival in harsh environments. Modern mind has far more advanced cognitive abilities, including complex language, symbolic thinking, creativity and problem thinking. The development of writing systems, art, culture, and technology has exponentially increased human's cognitive capacities.

Although, anatomically modern humans have existed for around 300,000 years, the mental capacities, cognitive skills and behaviors of early Homo sapiens differ significantly from those of modern humans due to cultural, environmental, and technological advances over time. Earlier, man used to live in small, tight-knit groups and their survival depended on cooperation.

While brain size hasn't changed much, the structure and functionality of the brain have evolved. The prefrontal cortex, responsible for higher order thinking, decision-making and complex social behaviors, is more refined. Human ability to abstract, imagine, and manipulate information has advanced significantly.

Language Development

There was no language, so our ancestors of pre-historic time were not able to expressions their feelings through words. The overall shape of the human brain had altered, but size remains almost the same as revealed from the scientific study of fossil skulls. Although, Homo sapiens emerged 200,000 years ago, the early language development dates back to 100,000 to 50,000 years ago. Earlier, only gestures and vocalizations were parts of proto-language.

Pre-historic humans minutely observed and mimicked bird songs, animal vocalizations, and body language to develop communication. Early mode of communication was inspired from many animals/plants. Many creatures communicate effectively using various vocalizations like grunts, groans, chirps and songs. These sounds convey vital information, facilitating social interaction, warning calls and even courtship.

The discovery and development of language were indeed ground-breaking in the evolution of human mind. Prior to this emergence of complex language, earlier humans had mental faculties that were more likely more similar to other animals. Pre-historic humans, like other animal counterparts, relied heavily on instincts, basic communication, and survival-driven behaviors. However, as language evolved, it became a powerful tool that fundamentally changed the way humans think, interact, and understand the world.

Charles Darwin in his book "The Descent of Man (1871) writes: "While other animals communicate through sounds, gestures, and expressions, humans have developed a more complex system of language. He argues that the development of language was crucial for evolution of advanced mental capabilities, such as abstract thought and awareness." The mind is part of the natural world, shaped by same evolutionary forces that influence physical traits.

The evolution of the human mind opened up limitless possibilities, making us capable of reshaping the world around us, even to the point where we have become masters of our environment and the forces of nature. The idea of time-travel is gaining momentum. The desire to go back in time and observe our ancestors, how they lived, hunted and adapted to their environment is rooted in our deep mind to understand our origins and evolution of man.

Comparative Study: Evolution of Mind

There are different approaches to study the development of human mind and each has a different assumptions and theory which may agree on some points or may not agree. It is common to different paths to trace the history of human evolution and how human evolved from apes. Homo sapiens or modern humans emerged in Africa with hunting as their sole source of food way back in 200,000 years ago.

The earliest human had simple cultures, but around 40,000 years ago, a big transformation was noticed which paved the way for complex cultures. Earlier nomadic people began to settle in one place and engaged in agricultural practices. As civilizations advanced with time, writing system emerged thus making the human mind thinker and visionary. Some researchers are of the view that it all happened owing to alteration in human cognition. Let's look what scientists, philosophers, linguists and spiritual text says about:

a. Noam Chomsky is American linguist, philosopher, cognitive scientist and historian all rolled into one. He has written extensively on the evolution of mind in the background of language development and human cognition. He stresses that language is a nature-gifted cognitive faculty unique to humans. His theory of a Universal Grammar conceives that the capacity for language is stored into the human brain. It suggests that humans are born with an inborn ability to acquire or learn language. That trait makes him apart from other species (that rely on sound and gestures to communicate).

b. According to Chomsky, language is not limited to communication only, but it also conveys your thoughts, emotions and feelings in most impressive way. He suggests that the language faculty may have emerged suddenly rather through a slow and gradual process. He adds that it may have happened due to minor genetic mutation.

c. Steven Pinker is a leading cognitive scientist has worked on how the mind works in different environment and how it reacts to stimuli. He has written extensively on the evolution of human mind in his famous book "How the Mind Works" and the "Blank Slate". He argues that the human mind, like the human body, is a product of natural selection. He believes that many of human cognitive capacities, emotions and behaviors have evolved to solve specific problems faced by our ancestors in the challenging environment of evolutionary adaptation.

d. Terrence Deacon, a biological anthropologist and neuroscientist explains the evolution of mind in different realm in his famous book "The Symbolic Species: The Co-evolution of language and the Brain." His work focuses on how the human brain in combination with mind evolved in conjunction with symbolic language, emphasizing the role of communication and culture in cognitive development. He believes that language and brain structure evolved together in a reciprocal process. The brain adapted to accommodate the demands of symbolic communication, and at the same time, language evolved as humans developed cognitive capacities.

e. *Sankhya* philosophy: Matter or nature evolves into multiple layers of worldly existence, including the mind. The mind (or manas) is seen as part of this material evolution, interacting with senses and intellect to experience the world.

f. In *Advaita Vedanta*, the evolution of mind is not seen as a physical or cognitive process, but as a process of realizing the true nature of the 'Self'.

g. Buddhist philosophy approaches the evolution of mind from a psychological and ethical standpoint, focusing on the impermanent and conditioned nature of mind which is always changing every moment.

h. *Kashmir Shaivism* speaks highly of universal consciousness as the ultimate reality of human and mind is only a utilitarian and a manifestation of subtlest consciousness.

The Isolation Paradox

What would happen to the mind of a person if his whole upbringing is carried out in complete isolation? Will he be a replica of Homo sapiens or modern world's scientific advancement would have some impact on his intelligence or IQ level? Mind learns from the environment (homely and educational institute), individual learning capabilities.

There are certain tribes like Jarawa tribe of Andaman Islands and Korwa tribe (Chhattisgarh) with limited contact are still dependent on hunting and faming to sustain life. The world has changed and we have entered into new millennia, but some tribes are still living a marginalized life--totally cut-off from the mainstream society.

A man left alone deep in the jungle might not have a complete blank mind (of a newborn child), because human mind evolves even in the absence of language and social interaction. Human beings have innate cognitive abilities, such as problem-solving, pattern recognition and basic survival instincts in his genome. These faculties allow a person to interact with and learn from the environment, even in the absence of formal language or social interaction.

The story of Ho Van Lang and his father is testimony of the above statement. The father-son duo fled to the deep jungle during the Vietnam War in the early 1970s after their inhabitant place was heavily bombed and several members of their family were killed in the war. Fearing their life, they fled in the jungle of the QuangNgai province, and remained isolated for four decades. They remained primitive in their outlook surviving on basic instincts.

While social interaction and language greatly enhance cognitive development, especially in terms of abstract thinking and complex knowledge transfer, the mind is not entirely dependent on these for all forms of learning. Humans are inherently social beings, and cognitive growth is deeply tied to collaboration, learning from others, and language acquisition.

Meeting new people and experiencing diverse cultures can indeed boost the evolution of mind by exposing individuals to different ideas, perspectives and ways of thinking. Israelis are known for their sharp and creative mind because they expand their mental horizons fostering broader understanding, innovation and adaptability.

The individual would likely develop their own strategies for survival, form some understanding of their environment and possibly even create a form of inner communication or thought pattern, albeit limited compared to a socially nurtured mind. When Lang and his father were rehabilitated to their native village way back in 2013, they found the world amazing.

The human mind is comprised of neurons, synapses and brain tissues and its evolution is shaped by millions of years of natural selection. It is influenced by environment and personal experiences. If you are living in traditional spiritual environment, the capability of mind's creativity and innovation will diminish and it will be replaced by spiritual bent of mind.

Both India and Israel got independence at the same time, but our country remained associated with mysticism and spiritual traditions. India's soil is enriched that saw the emergence of world known mystics like *Buddha*, *Mahavira*, *Adi Shankaracharya*, *Nanak*, *Kabir* and *Meera*. India gave value to enlightenment and salvation, instead of material or scientific advancement.

Israelis are known for their superb brain and creativity because they value science and technology at par with religious sentiments. Before Independence and even at first three decades post-Independence era, there were fewer platforms for scientific discovery and research. India was still struggling with poverty, poor infrastructure and economic instability. So, many scientists migrated to USA and other countries to prove their worth.

Modern Mind vs. Primitive Mind

Sigmund Freud says: "The primitive mind is guided by instinct, intuition and tradition." As we enter into space age, the man's instinctual wisdom fades, and it replaced by rational thoughts. Disconnected from primal instincts, the modern mind becomes unnatural, prioritizing logic over intuition. Lost in thoughts, the modern mind is disillusioned by empty promises, burdened by surplus information and disconnected from his/her essence.

To live in harmony with oneself and the roaming group was the need of primitive people. In search of food and protection from wild animals, they were always on the move. Sometimes, they travelled by day and by night. Their trip could have taken them through rivers and the streams. In that environment, there was little time for planning for the future. However, in modern times, physical and emotional demands are constantly placed upon many areas of life.

The modern mind is a highly self-centered, sensitive to the sense of dignity and importance of individual functions in the domestic domain and the public domain of the world of work. The modern man is rational in approach, careful in handling situations and want to do things as best as possible. The modern world loves a winner and every person is eager to prove himself. The modern mind is a labyrinth of lunacy, fragmented by information overload.

In close proximity with nature, the primitive mind dwelled in absolute simplicity. Undisturbed by desires, expectations or societal pressures, it found joy in eating, sleeping and procreation--the basic necessities of life. Contentment remained in the core of their heart, free from ambition, anxiety and existential complexity.

But there is brighter picture also. Modern mind is often seen as more logical, practical and visionary as compared to the primitive mind, largely due to the advancements in knowledge, technology and social structures over time. However, it's essential to recognize that this comparison doesn't imply an inherent superiority of modern thinking, but rather reflects the context in which each mind operates, where everything is available with the click of a mouse.

Logical thinking: Modern thinking emphasizes formal logic, scientific, reasoning and cultural thinking. The modern mind has access to centuries of accumulated knowledge and can apply systematic methodologies to problem-solving. In contrast, primitive societies relied more on instinct, myth and oral traditions for survival, which served their needs in their environment.

Long-term planning: Today's world is reined by scientific tools, educational institutions and policy-makers that allow for long-term planning and innovation. The primitive mind, however, was practical in a different sense--its focus was on immediate survival, resource management and community-based solutions. Time has changed, and so the priorities.

Visionary thinking: Modern minds can imagine a future shaped by technology, social reform and global inter connection. The tools we have today like science, communication networks, and date analysis helps us shape a vision of the future. However, even early humans had visionary thinking in the form of myths, religious beliefs and storytelling, which framed their understanding of life and the world.

Mind is a link between the outer world and the inner world, which is within you. It is a link between the modern and the primitive within you. It can be used to bridge two quite contradictory things--that which is inherited and that which is accumulated from the outer world. Outwardly you may differ from others, but inwardly we are the same. It happens because; we all belong to the same ancestors who had primitive mind.

The modern mind has developed tools and frameworks that allow us for different kinds of thinking, but the primitive mind was equally suited to the environment in which it existed, with its own strengths and adaptive thinking. Both have their place in the story of human evolution. Harmony lies in balancing primitive instinct and modern reasoning. Integrating intuition with intellect, nature with technology and heart with head is the need of the hour.

Factors that Influenced Human Intelligence

The idea that grip and tool use significantly contributed to human evolution has been the topic of discussion among scholars over time. However, one of the key figures to explore the bond between tool use and cognitive evolution is paleoanthropologist Louis Leakey. He along with his wife Mary in the discovery of early hominid fossils and tools in East Africa provided evidence backing the idea that tool use and manual dexterity were turning factors in human evolution.

Later, scientists like Jane Goodall added to this theory by observing tool use in primates, reinforcing the idea that the ability to maneuver objects was closely tied to the development of intelligence. Evolutionary advantage of bi-pedalism and the freeing of the hands for complex tasks were inevitable. The idea has also been supported by various researchers in evolutionary biology, anthropology and neuroscience such as Sherwood Washburn and Darwin.

The development of grip or the ability to hold and manipulate objects was undoubtedly a turning point in human evolution. This acquired trait allowed early humans to use tools effectively, which in turn motivated cognitive development and problem-solving abilities. With the use of sharp tools made from stone, humans could hunt more effectively, prepare food, build shelters and create art on the cave walls.

This also encouraged social cooperation and communication, laying the groundwork for more complex language and culture. The power of grip, therefore, played a significant role in shaping the human mind and thereby the society where he lived and prospered. The evolution of man is the replica of the evolution of the mind that highlights the parallel between physical evolution and the growth of human cognition.

The early man slowly learned to manipulate the surroundings to his own benefit, learned from the past experiences and predicted the outcome of his action and thereby cultivates ability to measure and calculate everything. Language evolved as a result of intelligence because in order to form sentences in understandable format, he needed the ability to manipulate words.

It suggests that as human beings evolved biologically, particularly with changes like bi-pedalism, tool use and brain expansion--these physical developments were mirrored by advancements in cognitive capabilities--such as language, abstract thought, problem-solving and social cooperation. Human mental evolution is intertwined with our physical evolution, with each influencing the other in a continuous loop of development.

Some may argue that chimpanzees also possess the power of grip, why this species could not advance in intelligence and higher thinking. While chimpanzees have the power of grip and some cognitive capabilities, but in humans, it was the combination of brain size, physical adaptation, social complexity and cultural advancement that made man what he is today.

- While chimpanzees have relatively large brains compared to other animals, but their brain size particularly the neocortex (responsible for refine thinking) is much smaller than that of humans

- Chimpanzees, while capable of using their hands as human do, are quadrupedal for much of their movement, which puts restriction on the wide variety of tasks they can perform with their hands
- Chimps have limited communication abilities (in absence of any language) compared to human

We may have landed on moon or planning township in the moon, but primitive fears rooted in early human evolution persist even in modern times, often manifesting in seemingly irrational ways like fear of dark, fear of snakes/spiders. These fears though less relevant in our technologically advanced societies, persists as remnants of our evolutionary past.

Michio Kaku, an American based theoretical physicist says: "Some people think that intelligence is the crowning achievement of evolution". Well, if that's true there should be more intelligent creatures on the planet earth. But to the best of our knowledge, we are the only ones. The dinosaurs were on the earth for roughly 200 million years and to the best of our knowledge not a single dinosaur became intelligent."

--OM--

Chapter 10

Balancing the Mind

Your mind is a mixed bag of joy and sorrow. You longs for joy; but sorrow comes without invitation. Everything perceived by the mind never stays forever. It fades and perishes from moment to moment. But it leaves imprint in your sub-conscious mind in the form of stress and burden. You need to confront negative or irrational thoughts, piercing emotions and feelings by identifying and replacing them with more balanced and positive perspectives.

There is no happiness in any object of the world reveals all spiritual texts. You imagine through your ignorance that you receive happiness from objects. On the contrary, the mind of the ignorant revolves in the world in the hope of achieving joy, peace and freedom. What you call world is only a 'thought'. Without mind, it has no existence. The same world evaporates in deep sleep and you experiences *indescribable* bliss and tranquility.

Life can be irksome if you are constantly consumed by worries and responsibilities. If you are too focused on work, family affairs and everyday concerns, you lose the ability to appreciate the simple beauty of life, like nature, and miss moments of peace. Balancing the mind involves inner peace, pure emotions and freedom from delusion or hallucination. A balanced mind does not turns gloomy in the midst of trials and tribulations.

Changing the State of Mind

Each of us is walking in his own mind. Your thoughts are distinct from my thoughts. Mind is the springboard of all your thoughts and apart from thoughts, mind is non-existent. Thoughts naturally appear in your mind without you making an effort to generate it. Thoughts come and go like the trains arrive and depart in a railway junction. Just as the breath flows effortlessly, thoughts can arise without forced mental effort.

The mind is everything. If the mind loses its balance, you lose yours. The mind, like a canvas, absorbs the colors of thoughts. Joy paints vibrant colors, sorrow shades grey, and fear tints dark. The continuously active chain of thoughts gravitates towards extremes. Attachment and detachment; love and hate; past and future--these polarities dominate your thoughts, emotions and experiences. Balancing the mind means color your mind wisely.

"A disturbed mind produces distorted thoughts," observed B. K. S. Iyengar. This is the source of all your problems and misery. In *ashtanga* yoga, "*yamas*" and *niyamas*" are practiced to tame the turbulent mind; but this is herculean task for normal man. The simple way is to tame your mind in such a way that it neither longs for anything nor does it reject anything. Only a free and undisturbed mind can understand that thoughts are just thoughts.An agitated mind, filled with anxiety and worry, makes it hard to relax or find simple joy in life. It can make you feel nervous, stressed and overly concerned with tasks and responsibilities.

युक्ताहारविहारस्य युक्तचेष्टस्य कर्मसु।
युक्तस्वप्नावबोधस्य योगो भवति दुःखहा। ।भगवद्गीता, 6.17। ।

Yoga becomes the destroyer of pain for him who is moderate in eating and recreation (such as walking, etc.), who is moderate in exertion in actions, who is moderate in sleep and wakefulness.

A balanced mind finds harmony between work and relaxation, allowing you to care for your responsibilities and also duties without being overwhelmed, and to pause and enjoy life's beauty along the way. Balance your thoughts and emotions, and you will achieve balance in life.

Cultivating a Balance Mind

What it means to cultivate a balance mind? It is a way of living that allows you to enjoy more aspects of your life in a more fulfilling way. It is about making specific choices that give you the opportunity to feel your best for as long as you can. It seems that there is a growing pressure to stay updated on every event happening around the globe, to be aware of every political, social and economic issue, and to keep pace with latest trends.

While staying informed is important, there is fundamental difference being aware of your surroundings and drowning in an excess of information. The truth is, there is no need to know every person or every happening around the world. What you need most is to live in the direct experience, grounded in the present moment, to cultivate a balanced mind.

And this balance cannot come from external sources; it must emerge from within. Direct experience refers to engaging with life in real time, as it unfolds. It is the raw, unfiltered interaction with the world through your senses, thoughts and feelings. This is how you make sense of your own existence. Direct experience could be something as simple as observing little kids playing with toys, chasing an energetic puppy in your lawn, eating with close-knitted family.

In contrast, overconsumption of information from external sources can lead to confusion, anxiety, and detachment from your immediate reality. When you try to follow every event happening worldwide, you become overwhelmed. The delicate human mind is not designed to process the vast amount of information available at your fingertips today.

Trying to know more and more can lead to a scattered mind, making it harder to focus on what truly matters. The pursuit of encyclopedic knowledge, while valuable, often distracts you from the vital aspect of your existence i.e. inner balance. Inner balance refers to a state of mental and emotional balance that allows you to respond to life with clarity and calmness.

If you want to live a healthy lifestyle, you need to manage the information in your life so that it doesn't overtake you. This means taking charge of your thoughts, emotions, tasks and environment to get your mind in balance. This balance cannot be achieved by absorbing more and more external information. Instead, it requires a deliberate inward focus, a connection to your inner world, and an understanding of your thoughts and emotions.

An unbalanced mind is like a roaring sea, tossing thoughts and emotions without rest. If you constantly feed mind with endless streams of information without discernment, it becomes cluttered and chaotic. To cultivate a balanced mind, you need to push away unnecessary distractions and focus on blooming inner petals of life. This involves setting boundaries and engaging hobbies without losing the balance of mind.

These simple practices help you observe your thoughts without judgment, allowing you to gain insights into your own mental patterns. Living in the present moment is one of the most powerful tools for creating inner balance without getting lost in past regrets or future anxieties. In this way, you stop chasing after piece of information.

Another key aspect of inner balance is learning to let go of the need to control everything, including the flow of information. Many of you feel the urge to stay on top for all worldly information because it gives you sense of well-informed man. But the reality is, no matter how much you know, you can't be the knower of each and every thing.

Research has shown that a man with unbalanced mind cannot concentrate, he cannot absorb what he is reading, and he cannot make calculations and make mistakes. Letting go means accepting the limits of your knowledge and focusing on what is within your sphere of influence--your actions, attitudes and responses to the present moment. By releasing the need to know everything, you free yourselves from unnecessary mental burdens and open up.

Causes of Mental Instability

Before attaining inner calmness, it is crucial to understand the causes of mental instability because addressing the root of the problem is must for lasting solutions. Without knowing the underlying causes, any attempt at mental balance might be wild goose chase, like a doctor treating symptoms without diagnosing the illness. It can result in a cycle of short relief followed by repeated episodes of instability.

By knowing the causes of emotional upheaval, whether they offshoot from external factors like a stressful working environment or inner conflicts such as suppressed emotions or negative thinking patterns, individuals can take required steps to address these issues. Moreover, understanding the causes of mental instability helps prevent recurrence. If one is aware of the triggers that lead to emotional or psychological instability, these can be managed effectively.

Disbalance in the mind can have horrible impact on a person's psyche, affecting his emotional, mental and even physical well-being. Several factors contribute to mental instability, and considering these causes is essential for developing coping mechanism and strategies to maintain balance. Here are some chief causes for mental instability:

Lack of interest in work: A lack of interest in work can lead to a sense of purposelessness, boredom and frustration. Remember that work is not merely a means of earning a livelihood; for many; it provides a sense of purpose, satisfaction, identity and contentment. When there is a lack of motivation or interest in the work one is doing, the whole life seems to be dog-dragging. This disinterest can trigger from various sources like monotony, the feeling that the work is worthless, lack of praise or appreciation from immediate boss, and low paid salary. Over time, this sense of apathy can snowball into depression or psychological strain.

Lord Krishna clearly declares in Shrimad *Bhagvad Gita:*

न मे पार्थास्ति कर्तव्यं त्रिषु लोकेषु किञ्चन।
नानवाप्तमवाप्तव्यं वर्त एव च कर्मणि।।3.22।।

I have no personal grounds to engage myself in action. I have nothing to achieve as I have all divine wealth and yet I engage myself in action. Why do you not follow my example? Why do you not endeavour to prevent the masses from following the wrong path by setting an example yourself? If you set an example, people will follow you as you are a leader with noble alities.

When people fail to find meaning in their daily routines, their minds start to roam toward negative thinking, self-doubt and low self-esteem. This inner conflict not only affects their professional life but also seeps into personal relationships, social interactions and overall mental health. Restoring balance in this situation involves purpose and passion in one's chosen work or exploring parallel career options that align with personal values and goals.

Materialistic mindset: A materialistic mindset focuses heavily on the acquisition of wealth, possessions and status symbols. In a consumer-driven society, it is easy to fail into the equating happiness and success with material wealth. However, an overemphasis on materialistic possessions provides only temporary satisfaction and the desire for more leads to never ending state of wanting or yearning. This hedonic treadmill causes individuals to constantly chase after the next big thing, leaving them unfulfilled on the long run.

Materialism also triggers competition, jealousy, and comparison with others. When one's self-worth is tied to external factors like money, cars, houses or luxury items, emotional vigor becomes fragile. Financial setbacks or a perceived instability to keep up with others can cause anxiety, stress and feelings of rejection. Breaking free from this mindset and shifting focus toward intrinsic values such as relationships and personal growth can restore mental balance.

Disturbed home environment: It is a crucial factor in inner peace. A home should ideally be a place of peace, security and emotional support. However, when there is constant conflict, fight or instability within the four walls of a room, it becomes a breeding ground for mental instability. Disturbed home environments can result from marital issues, poor communication, financial stress or untimely death of loved ones.

Children growing up in such stressful milieu often carry emotional scars into adulthood, affecting their ability to form healthy relationships with their peer group and manage stress. Living in a chaotic home environment can lead to anxiety, depression and emotional exhaustion. The lack of a safe emotional space prevents individuals from decompressing after stressful events, thereby further worsening mental instability.

Addressing issues within the home, seeking counseling (if required) or creating an environment of open communication can help mitigate these negative effects and restore mental stability. Last but not the least, Tulsidas writes in *Ramcharitmanas*: "No distress or worry can affect the mind of one who remembers God" (*mana ke dukha kaha na hoye, jo simran kare prabhu soye*).

Attaining Equilibrium State of Mind

You must awake your conscience and soul to understand the equilibrium state of mind. Let you not temper with either your own nature or that of the Supreme. Kabir Das says: "Don't speak too much good, don't keep silent too much. Too much rain is not good; too much sunshine is not good." In simple words, excess of anything is dreadful.

Everybody's mind becomes concentrated at times. You all concentrate upon those things you love, and you love those things upon which you concentrate your mind. The great trouble with such concentration is that you don't control the mind; it controls you. Avoiding extremes like love and hate, praise and criticism can contribute to mental stability by promoting emotional balance, deeper understanding and nurturing a mindset of acceptance.

Extreme emotions like intense love or hatred can paralyze the mind. Love, in extreme form, might lead to an unhealthy attachment where one's sense of self becomes overly dependent on another person. Your circumstances and conditions are not dictated by the world outside; it is the inner world within you that creates outside.

On the other hand, extreme hate can consume a person, inviting resentment, anger and negativity, which are mentally draining emotions. Beyond love and hate's polarized dance, lies a realm of profound acceptance. Transcend emotional extremes, and discover inner peace, unwavering calm and unconditional compassion.

Similarly, extremes in perception such as always seeking praise and avoiding criticism can create an unstable self-image. Praise can boost one's confidence, but when relied on excessively, it becomes a crutch that leads to insecurity when it's absent. If one defines their worth based solely on external approval, they risk feelings inadequate when that approval isn't forthcoming. On the flip side, harsh criticism or an excessive focus on it can lead to self-doubt, which hinders growth and develops a negative self-image.

Likewise, viewing relationships in black-and-white terms, categorizing people strictly as friends and foes, limits the complexity of human connections. In the fleeting dance of life, no one is permanent friend or enemy. Relationships shift like sands, driven by circumstances. Let go of labels, cultivate compassion and see the same divine in every human-being.

If someone is always seen as an ally or enemy, it closes off the possibility of understanding the gray areas in relationships. Even those you consider friends may sometimes hurt you and those you perceive as enemies may act kindly. Allowing room for these nuances promotes healthier relationships and prevents feelings of betrayal or unwarranted animosity.

Mental stability often depends on balance. Emotional and cognitive equilibrium is essential to maintain a clear perspective on life's challenges and relationships. Extremes disrupt this balance by pulling the mind in diagrammatically opposing directions. In contrast, maintaining a moderate stance allows one to flow with life's ups and downs more smoothly.

Regarding hate, tempering negative emotions enables a person to approach conflicts with a calm, rational mindset. By avoiding extremes, they can address issues with empathy and understanding, reducing the potential for stress and frustration. This is not to suggest suppressing anger or discomfort but rather managing these feelings in a way that they don't dominate one's emotional space.

A balanced approach to praise and criticism also helps in mental stability. Learning to accept praise graciously is one of the cornerstones of happiness. Similarly, viewing criticism as constructive rather than harmful enables personal growth. Both feedback forms are necessary, but relying on either too heavily can distort one's sense of self.

Man's ultimate goal should be attainment of true happiness. But the way to attain this happiness is not easy or smooth. The human beings should avoid the extreme in everything. Moreover, seeing people beyond simple categories of friends and foes allows for more meaningful and flexible relationships.

Living a Fruitful Life

It is a desire shared by many, yet the path toward achieving it is often filled with challenges. The key to unlocking a life of worthy is through the balance of mind and thoughts. Your thoughts are mirror of your reality. What you think and how you react determines the quality of your life, shaping your perceptions, emotions, actions and ultimately, your destiny.

Learning to cultivate and balance your thoughts is the foundation for living a life rich in purpose and meaning. Several historical figures are considered to have demonstrated a remarkable balance of mind, often, due to their wisdom, calm, demeanor and ability to maintain inner harmony in the face of challenges.

Buddha is perhaps the most iconic figure associated with achieving perfect balance of mind. He preached the middle path that refers to balanced approach to spiritual practice that avoids the extremes of self-indulgence and self-mortification. Whatever he does, he moves to the source consciously, alert and aware. His serenity and compassion are hallmarks of a balanced mind.

Your thoughts are like seeds you plant in the garden of your mind. Just as a gardener carefully select the seeds to grow, you must be mindful of the thoughts you allow to take root. Positive, constructive thoughts can lead to growth, peace and fulfillment, while negative destructive thoughts can produce feelings of despair, anger or confusion.

The act of balancing your thoughts is akin to nurturing the mental garden with utmost care and attention. By doing so, you create an environment that is conducive to a meaningful and harmonious life. Lao Tzu, the founder of Taoism, emphasizes living in the harmony with the Tao (the way of nature) advocating a life of simplicity, humility and balance.

Balancing the mind begins with awareness. Many of you might go through life on autopilot, reacting to circumstances and situations, without pausing to examine the underlying thoughts that drive your emotions and behaviors. This mechanical approach often leads to unnecessary stress and turmoil. However, when you practice mindfulness and self-awareness, you begin to notice patterns in your thinking.

You become conscious of the recurring, limiting thoughts that hold you back, as well as empowering beliefs that move you forward. With this awareness, you can begin to intentionally shift your thinking in ways that promote balance and feel good factor.

One crucial aspect of balancing your thoughts is, understanding the relationship between the mind and emotions. Thoughts are not isolated entities; they are deeply tied with your emotional state. A negative thought can trigger a cascade of emotions, which if left unchecked, can spiral into anxiety or depression.

Conversely, positive and balanced thinking can lead to feelings of peace, contentment and joy. To live a fruitful life, you must learn to manage this interplay between thoughts and emotions. This means recognizing when your thoughts are creating unnecessary emotional turmoil and then consciously choosing to shift your focus.

Many people find themselves trapped in a cycle of future's worry and over-thinking, constantly dwelling on problems or uncertainties. This mental fixation on things outside of your control can lead to feelings of helplessness and frustration. However, by cultivating acceptance and detachment, you free yourself from this vicious cycle.

You are not thoughts. Thoughts can be managed and transformed. It is also important to cultivate positive and affirmative thoughts. This doesn't mean ignoring challenges or avoiding difficult emotions, but rather approaching life with a mindset of optimism and possibility. When you face obstacles, instead of succumbing to negative thinking, you can choose to see them as opportunities for growth.

Living a fruitful life requires intentional effort to balance your thoughts. Your mind is the mirror through which you perceive the world, and by mastering your thinking, you can shape a life filled with purpose, peace and fulfillment. This balance is achieved through awareness, emotional regulation, acceptance and the conscious cultivation of positive thoughts. Efforts lead to attainment.

Stay Balanced in Challenging Situations

There is no end to confronting difficult situation every now and then. The problem may appear hard and depressing, but there is a way out. Staying grounded and maintains a composed demeanor, especially when the mind is agitated, requires time-tested traditional techniques and strategies. Here are some tips to help you stay balanced in challenging situations:

Breathing awareness: You become frustrated or hopeless, be aware of your breath. In agitated state of mind, breath flows rapidly. Yoga reveals that breath and mind are interconnected. In calm and balanced state of mind, breath flows equally from both nostrils.

Some people presume that inner world is meant for hermits, monks and reclusive. Indian awakened yogis have decoded many mysteries of mind and revealed that mind and breath are interconnected. If you pacify the breath, the mind will automatically will come under your control.

Reframe the Situation: The external world is not the cause of your anger, frustration and mood swings. All the negativity is within you, the outer circumstances only trigger the suppressed emotions. When you face any such situation, don't react instead shift your perspective. Rather than reacting to the external event, ask yourself: "What's the worst that could happen to me?" All events are short-lived, the come and go like the waves of the sea. This reaction helps lower the emotional intensity and bring a sense of control.

Grounding techniques: No situation can live for longer as life is changing moment to moment. Don't fritter away your energy in focusing yourself in an imaginary worst situation. When old bad memories come in mind as flashbacks, focus on the present moment. Engage your senses by noticing the things around you. For example, identify five things related to your cognitive senses that you can touch, smell, or see. This grounds your mind in the present moment.

Focus on what you can control: When confronted with erratic man using foul language, you need to stay calm, composed and empathetic. Set boundaries firmly and don't engage or react. Seek help (only if threatened or there is impending danger to your life). When faced with complex situations, remind yourself to focus on the aspects you can control and let go of those you cannot. This helps reduce stress and frustration.

Take a break: All human behavior is driven by the desire to seek happiness and avoid challenging situation. But good and bad phases of life are harsh reality of life. When you feel situation is going out of your control, step away for a moment. Even a short walk or change of environment can help reset your mind, reducing agitation.

Keep a mental anchor: Use a mental anchor to calm and focus your mind in challenging situation. Breathe deeply and evenly without losing the balance of your mind. Have a mental "safe space" or a specific mantra you can return to when feeling distressed. Something like "This too shall pass" or "I am calm and in control" can help center your thoughts.

Staying Unruffled through Inner Cleansing

Staying unruffled or staying grounded in the face of life's unavoidable ups and downs is a deeply spiritual practice that makes you stronger mentally and emotionally. Through consistent practice and witnessing awareness, you can learn that true strength lies not in controlling external circumstances but in cultivating calm, clear and remaining level-headed. Inner purity can lead you to mental and emotional balance through faith and compassion.

Much like a gardener tends to a field, removing weeds and cultivating flowers, individuals must actively clear the "weeds" from their minds to maintain poise. These weeds can take the form of fear, anger, doubt and other negative emotions that if left unchecked, can create havoc in your inner world. By adopting pragmatic approach, one can promote clarity, wisdom and grace, ensuring a harmonious inner world.

Just as a neglected field can become overgrown and wild without attention, the human mind, left unchecked, can become cluttered with negative thoughts and emotions. Fear, anger and doubt are invasive plants that take root deep in your consciousness. These emotions grow stronger over time, fed by your insecurities and past experiences. Without awareness, they can dominate your inner space, leading to anxiety and unrest.

In spiritual science, it is often preached that the root cause of most negativity comes from a polluted or clouded inner consciousness. This happens when the mind becomes off-track by external circumstances, worldly attachments and ego-driven desires. When you focus too much on what you fear, on what anger you, or on self-doubt, you block your ability to connect with pure consciousness. You allow negativity to dictate your thoughts and actions.

In this way, you are much like the gardener who faces the daunting task of clearing a field overrun by weeds. To regain control of your mental and emotional space, you must recognize these harmful patterns. Alertness is the first step: taking stock of your emotional responses, examining the origins of your fears and doubts, and acknowledging when anger begins to grow. This self-awareness acts as a gardener's hands, gently identifying and pulling out the weeds before they can grow too strong.

One cannot simply weed a garden once and expect it to remain clear forever. Life's challenges continually give rise to new emotions, and it is an ongoing process to cultivate and maintain inner peace. By simply noticing a feeling like fear without judgment, you give yourself space to choose a response rather than automatically react.

Fear, anger, doubt and other negative emotions are not a part of your inner space. They trespass only when you allow it (knowingly or unknowingly). Jim Corbett in his famous book *Man-Eaters of Kumaon* writes that "man-eaters often turn to human flesh due to injury, old age or lack of natural food sources." When you live in harmony with your essential nature, you recognize that all experiences, whether pleasant or challenging, serve a purpose.

The role of spirituality in this process is insightful. It teaches that your true essence lies beyond the fleeting emotions of fear, anger or doubt. When you connect with the deeper aspects of your being, you come to know that these emotions are temporary visitors, not permanent dwellers of your inner space. By tuning into this higher consciousness, you tap into an infinite source of wisdom and calm, allowing you to face life's challenges with dignity.

Balancing the mind and experiencing its ruffling is a fundamental dichotomy of life. The human mind is prone to oscillating between states of clarity and focus; and confusion and distraction. Thoughts can easily divert attention from a chosen path, whether it is simple task or a greater life goal. Life is a flow between extremes--between joy and sorrow, focus and distraction. However, the essence of life lies in understanding these fluctuations and training yourself to remain aware, even you don't remain collected. This awareness of the mind's distraction is the first step towards staying calm under pressure.

Life is not a straight path but a serpentine road filled with obstacles and unexpected turns. Yet, the beauty of life lies in exploring these challenges with utmost care and alertness. Though one may struggle initially, they key is persistence, for consistent practice leads to mastery, and this journey is the true essence of life. The pursuit of balance, whether mental or otherwise, is not about achieving a state of perfection but about rising from the dust like phoenix.

The essence of life, in fact, lies in this balance between two contractions. Life is not about ever getting distracted, but about learning to come back to the centre whenever and wherever distraction occurs. Life is a practice--a continual process of realigning oneself with one's purpose, values and focus. It is a lifelong practice, and its occasional dis-balance is not a failure but an opportunity for growth and transformation.

---OM---

Chapter 11

Power of Human Mind

The power of the mind has been a central question in philosophy for centuries, and modern philosophers continue to grapple with its implications. When you harness the power of mind efficiently, it can lead to incredible individual transformation. However, if misused or left unchecked, it can lead to self-doubt, pessimism and questionable behaviors. Modern thinkers are exploring this further to understand how we can better cultivate human minds?

A person with a focused mind and determined will can control the entire universe. Mind has the power to shape your destiny and by controlling your thoughts and emotions, you can achieve greatness. In a material world, a focused mind can help you to win the Nobel Prize and in spiritual domain, it can lead you to 'enlightenment'. Mind has the potential to be a powerful tool for transformation and liberation.

From the dawn of human evolution, the mind has been the driving force behind your survival, innovation and growth. What began as a tool for survival--helping early humans to hunt, gather and protect them--has evolved into something more sophisticated and transformative. Today, the human mind has gone far beyond the mere process of survival. It now seeks purpose, creativity and expansion in way that are limitless beyond imagination.

At its core, the mind possesses an inherent longing to expand, explore and evolve. This drive to explore is no longer constrained to physical necessities like food, shelter and safety. It is now directed towards abstract, intellectual and emotional dimensions of existence. As a human being, the mere fact of existence that keeps us alive no longer satisfies anyone. The individual desire has shifted towards personal fulfillment, intellectual discovery and creative expression.

This shift in the mind's function can be attributed to the evolutionary process of humanity. As societies evolved and the past pressure of survival decreased, humans began to invest more energy into pursuits that were not directly related to survival but were instead connected to exploring new dimensions of the mind and existence. This gave rise to art, science, philosophy and other streams of knowledge.

The mind is no longer content with just surviving; it seeks to thrive, to understand its place in the universe, and to leave a footprint that extends far beyond individual lifetimes. One of the most captivating aspects of the human mind is its ability to harness infinite potential. The mind is not limited to gross constraints; it can think in abstract terms, imagine scenarios that don't yet exist, and bring those ideas to life.

This is evident in human ability to create poetry, art and music--forms of expression that transcend the physical world and tap into something deeply emotional and metaphysical. The act of painting, for instance, allows the mind to manifest its visions on canvas, blending imagination and reality. Similarly, poems channel the mind's thoughts and feelings into words that can evoke powerful emotions and ideas.

In the field of science, the human mind has made stupendous success from unraveling the mysteries of the universe to engineering technological marvels. A programmer, for instance, uses the power of the analytical mind to create intricate systems of logic that govern the digital mind, opening new vistas for innovation.

Scientists uses their intelligence to explore the natural world and uncover the truths about mysteries of nature, while astronauts represent the physical manifestation of the mind's desire to reach beyond the boundaries of our planet and explore the cosmos. What makes all of this possible is the mind's tremendous capacity for growth and learning.

There are millions of spaces in your mind which are magical. Human mind in its evolutionary journey have gathered so many dimensions. The possibilities are endless; the mind can shape reality, explore new dimensions, and create worlds that only exist in the realm of imagination. The challenge lies not in finding this power but in learning how to harness it fully.

Contemplative Power of Mind

The power of creation is the innate power of every individual. It's not that only Einstein, Edison, Newton, Aryabhatta, Carl Sagan or Ramanujan had genius mind, you too can create whatever you imagine or contemplate. Whatever you dream or desire is already in existence; otherwise it can't arise in the space of your mind. You only need to integrate unrelated concepts.

The human mind is an intricate and power entity, holding vast untapped potential within its depths. It's often said that only a small fraction of your mental capacity is used in daily life. Popular anecdotes suggest that Albert Einstein used merely two percent of his brain's full capacity. The mind's potential is vast, yet it remains untapped for most people. Imagine what humanity could achieve if more and more people engaged deeply with their mental powers.

The subconscious mind contains untapped resources, memories, and abilities that many never explore. Your mental reservoir includes your thoughts, emotions, creativity, and the limitless capacity to learn and adapt. This potential often goes dormant simply because you haven't learned how to access it.

In reality, the mind operates as a powerful tool for creating your experiences. Every invention, from the wheel to space voyage, was born from human thought and imagination. The mind has the ability to visualize possibilities and bring them into reality through persistent effort. Thomas Edison once told reporters: "Genius is 1 % inspiration and 99 % perspiration."

This capacity for creativity and abstract thought is unique to humanity. And yet, many people remain unaware of this power, limiting their lives to the constraints of habit, routine, and societal expectations. Imagination is the stepping-stone to creativity in every stream of knowledge. What you need is thinking outside the box.

Imagination is not day-dreaming. It is gateway to ideas, innovation and higher awareness. Albert Einstein used to interconnected knowledge across physics, math and philosophy and his habit of playing on piano also contributed in synthesizing data to draw scientific conclusions. He visualized complex concepts in his famous "Theory of Relativity."

Similarly, Newton had analytical mind that helped him to break-down complex mathematical problems into easy understandable smaller parts. Newton was known for insatiable curiosity, strong intuition and clear visualization that made him genius. Imagination allows you to perceive realities that don't yet exist, giving you the first glimpse into new horizons.

For astrophysicist Carl Sagan, visualization was fun for him. He saw the unseen part of the universe that was mystery for others. Visualization is a focused, deliberate form of imagination that strengthens your connection to your goals and aspirations. Athletes, artists, and even successful entrepreneurs use visualizations techniques to achieve peak performance.

Let make you mind flying above the defined boundaries and rise above the ordinary. The analogy of an eagle flying above the clouds is a fitting example of the mind's potential. Eagles soar high, using the power of its wings when it rains. Likewise, you can harness your mental capacities; you can rise above the mundane limitations that cloud your lives.

There are innumerable dimensions of awareness, and one can reach anywhere just by breaking the wall of normalcy. Mind expands when ignorance's wall crumble, unleashing potential. Curiosity, passion for learning, and creative contemplation dissolve self-imposed limitations, illumining new perspectives and unlocking human potential's vast expanse.

Repositories of Knowledge

Genius minds inspire admiration worldwide, but there's a special pride in sharing a homeland with such individuals. Genius is the exceptional power of the mind, where deep focus, memory and creative converge, and allowing people to innovate and excel in their fields. Whether in science, art, literature or philosophy, these individuals see connections others might miss, bringing transformative ideas to life.

The incredible capacity of memory has captivated people for centuries. While many individuals read, learn and soon forget much of what they have encountered, some geniuses in human history have displayed exceptional memory, leaving indelible impressions in various fields. Their achievements, driven by relentless curiosity and mental acuity, contribute not only to individual success but also to societal progress.

Stalwarts like Swami Vivekananda, I. C. Vidyasagar, Osho, Kripalu ji maharaj and Rambhadracharya are prime examples, each demonstrating remarkable memory abilities that intensified their influence and their unique abilities have garnered global recognition and admiration. Their influence is felt everywhere in India but their significance is also great in the evolutionary phase of India.

Swami Vivekananda, one of India's most revered spiritual leaders, was a voracious reader known to read a large book in single sitting. His ability to recall everything he read with photographic precision allowed him to access information instantly and delivered powerful speeches that were both insightful and profound. This extraordinary forte not only enhanced his knowledge base but also made him a magnetic orator, drawing audiences around the globe. His photographic memory allowed him to retain every sentence he read, empowering him to quote texts verbatim, a skill that deeply influenced his listeners, and gave his discourses authenticity and authority.

Ishwar Chandra Vidyasagar was known for his remarkable memory, often described as photographic. He had an amazing memory to retain everything he read in a single glance. This talent deeply contributed to his scholarship and mastery of various subjects, including Sanskrit, English, Bengali and mathematics. His sharp memory and intellect were instrumental in his contributions to Indian education and social reformation.

Another notable figure is Osho, a world known spiritual leader who read nearly 1.5 lakh books over his lifetime. He was known for his encyclopedic knowledge across diverse domains, from philosophy and psychology to religion and science. What made Osho unique was not only his vast memory but his talent for synthesizing complex concepts into clear and relatable language. He simplifies the profound teaching of the Vedanta, Upanishads and other spiritual philosophy for the common parlance, making traditional wisdom accessible to contemporary audiences. He made connections between diverse subjects, comparing religious teachings with modern psychology, explaining spirituality in the language of science. This cross-disciplinary approach resonated with people around the world, particularly with those truth seekers looking for deeper meaning in their lives outside traditional religious frameworks. His ability to quote, interprets, and compare texts on the spot allowed him to build a bridge between ancient philosophers and the modern logical mind.

Jagadguru Kripalu Ji Maharaj, founder of Jagadguru Kripalu Parishat, was also known for his remarkable memory. He had an amazing memory to retain everything he read in a single glance. This talent deeply contributed to his scholarship and mastery of all *Vedas, Upanishads* in Sanskrit and Hindi. His sharp memory and intellect were instrumental in his contributions to reveal the true philosophy from the Vedic scriptures to mankind in the simplest form possible so that they may attain their true goal of God Realisation.

In the realm of Hindu religion, one of the most remarkable examples of genius minds is Jagadguru Rambhadracharya. Despite being blind since infancy, he memorized an astonishing number of religious texts and scriptures, becoming an authority on Hindu spiritual literature. His capacity to remember and recite complex texts like the *Vedas, Upanishads* and the *Ramayana* without sight is astonishing—a feat that would be difficult even for someone with vision.

Main Factors behind Tremendous Power of Mind

The human mind, undoubtedly, the powerhouse of knowledge, understanding and memory, is shaped by numerous factors. Each feature, from genetic make-up to neural connectivity, plays a vital role in determining an individual's mental capabilities. Knowing these factors gives you insights into tapping and maximizing mental power for personal and professional growth.

Purity of mind: Purity of mind is the cornerstone of maximizing mental power for personal growth. A pure mind is free from the clutter of negative emotions—such as anger, greed, jealousy, and ego—that cloud our true nature. When the mind becomes calm and unburdened, it starts reflecting the soul's innate qualities like love, compassion, and truth. Just as clean water reflects the sky above, a pure mind reflects the divine within. This purity is not achieved through suppression, but through awareness, self-reflection, and a sincere desire for inner transformation. True spirituality begins not in rituals or doctrines, but in the quiet cleansing of one's own thoughts. In cultivating purity of mind, we take our first step toward lasting joy and discovering the real potential of the human mind.

Genetic Make-up: It lays the basis of cognitive abilities, influencing aspects such as memory, intelligence, and personality traits. While genetic factors determine the brain's basic structure and functional potential, they are not absolute. Environmental influences, lifestyle choices, and individual effort can shape and mold one's cognitive abilities, illustrating the interplay between nature and nurture. In simple words, while genes may set the initial parameters, they do not rigidity define a person's potential, allowing space for growth and adaptation.

Non-stop learning: Learning is a continuous process that shapes your intelligence and IQ level. Engaging in non-stop learning exposes the mind to update information, enhances problem-solving ability and sharpens mental flexibility. It has been proved that consistent learning activities such as reading, practicing new skills or acquiring new knowledge, helps in strengthening neural connections and form new ones too. This plasticity allows the mind to adapt to new challenges and enhances its capacity to process information effectively, making learning a central factor in developing mental strength.

Time management: Effective time management is crucial for optimizing mental energy. When individuals allocate time wisely, they are better able to focus, manage stress and avoid mental fatigue. Effective time management not only increases productivity but also prevents cognitive overload. It allows individuals to prioritize tasks, focus on main goals, and create room for essential activities like relaxation, sleep and exercise, all of which contribute to mental well-being. The ability to structure time effectively boosts mental clarity, enabling the mind to function more efficiently.

Focus & concentration: Focus and concentration are must for achieving gravity in critical thinking and analysis. When individuals train themselves to focus, then enhance their ability to block out irrelevant information, sharpening their power of understanding and memory retention. Practicing total focus in chosen any activity such as reading, learning or writing notes can improve focus and concentration with time. Developing this discipline enhances cognitive processing and maximizes mental efficiency.

Sharp understanding: It allows individuals to process and interpret information accurately and speedily. It involves not only grasping facts but also discerning underlying patterns, making connections and synthesizing knowledge from various sources. This ability, often attributed to intelligence, enables people to approach complex situations with clarity and insight. Sharp understanding can be cultivated through critical thinking exercises, questioning assumptions and engaging in activities that challenge cognitive boundaries.

Access to resources: It includes educational materials, library, technology and social networks that play a important role in mental development. Resources expand the mental horizon of what individuals can learn and achieve. For example, access to books, online library or guidance of subject experts enhances knowledge acquisition and skill development. Technology also enables efficient learning through data analysis, virtual stimulations and diverse information resources. The presence of support systems and guidance can provide motivation and open doors to new opportunities, thereby sharpening your mental power.

Goal setting and planning: Having clear-defined goals provide a sense of direction, while planning offers a structured path to achieve them. Goal setting involves identifying what aims to accomplish, while planning outlines the steps necessary to reach their goal. Together, they create motivation, build discipline, and encourage perseverance. Goal-oriented individuals tend to be more focused and determined, as their mental energy is channeled toward achieving specific outcomes. This not only boosts productivity but also reinforces a positive mental framework that promotes learning with least effort.

Strength of neural connections: The strength and quality of neural connections play a fundamental role in cognitive power. Strong connections facilitate faster communication between neurons, allowing for quicker thought processing, memory retention and complex thinking. Neural plasticity, or the brain's ability to form new connections, is crucial for learning and adapting to new information. Physical exercise like yoga or jogging, sufficient sound sleep, and mental stimulation all support the strengthening of these connections.

Thus, we can say that mind's tremendous power is not solely the outcome of innate talent or intelligence; it's a product of a multifaceted approach-encompassing genetics, continuous learning, time-management, focus, sharp understanding, access to resources, goal setting and neural strength. By nurturing each of these factors, individuals can unlock their hidden mental potential, enabling them to overcome challenges, achieve their goals and continuously grow.

Imagine the Impossible

You can imagine only what you have experienced or perceive through the senses. It's need the exemplary courage to bend the rules of ordinary mind. If you look back into past, you will discover that human progress has often hinged on breaking conventions and daring to imagine the unimaginable. While most of the people loves to think in defined pattern, but it can also create mental barriers that restrict creativity and innovation.

Bending the rules and imagining the impossible are vital to unlocking new paths to success that have the potential to redefine industries, ideas, and entire societies. Most people think within familiar patterns--either because they are comfortable or because they are unaware of think differently. Traditional approaches are influenced by education, social background and established norms, creating a framework that we naturally default to.

For instance, a good orator will teach the traditional skills to would-be orators by reading, listening and aping renowned orators in the beginning to make their unique style later. But groundbreaking success requires us to question the adequacy of such approaches. Innovation doesn't typically emerge from repeating past successes or following safe methods; it comes from a willingness to bend, break, or even abandon those norms when necessary.

Imagination is central to this process. When we dare to imagine the unimaginable, we allow ourselves to seek diverse perspectives. Take the classic example of Wright brothers or Nikola Tesla. When Wright brother shared the idea, others made fun of them by saying that how a heavier machine can fly in the air.

However, by rethinking aerodynamics and rethinking the paradigm, they achieved what had previously been inconceivable. Similarly, Tesla imagined wireless electricity transfer at a time when the concept of wireless communication was itself groundbreaking. His ideas may have seemed fantastical, yet they laid the foundation of future innovations in energy and communication.

Another example comes from the field of technology and entrepreneurship. Take Elon Musk's ventures in space travel and electric vehicles. Musk's companies, like SpaceX and Tesla, were initially considered unfeasible. Musk's pursuit of reusable rockets or mass-market electric cars defied long-standing industry beliefs and required bending the norms in both design and operational practices. SpaceX achieved lower costs in space exploration by reimagining rocket production and reducing alliance on traditional suppliers.

Even in everyday life, this mindset of bending the rules and imagining the unimaginable can be transformative. Consider someone who finds themselves in a challenging situation, whether it's a financial crisis or a health issue. The typical response might be to follow prescribed solutions or look to common sources of advice. However, by questioning the standard approach, they may discover alternatives that can better meet their needs.

In a nutshell, achieving something different, something remarkable, requires us to break free from the boundary we have come to accept. It's about cultivating the courage to question, to experiment, and to entertain ideas that might seem impossible at first. True progress stems from individuals who dare to rethink the rules and consider new avenues.

Power of Silence

The mind, much like physical elements in the material world, thrives on activity and purpose. When iron is left unused, it rusts, losing both its shine and structural integrity. Similarly, stagnant water loses its purity and colorless and odorless properties. In the same way, when mind is overloaded with irrelevant thoughts becomes clouded losing its clarity.

When you spend your mental energy on trivial or repetitive worries, anxieties and distractions, you sap the vigor of mind, diminishing its potential for creativity, problem-solving and insight. Arjuna's mind was facing the same problems as he enters the battlefield on seeing his friends, relatives, near and dear ones and gurus. But Krishna mould his mind by his preaching.

The mind thrives in an environment where it's actively challenged, enriched and given moments of rest, much like the muscles in your body that grow stronger and more flexible with regular exercise but can weaken with overuse or neglect. Use your mind or waste it. Mind is a tool meant for growth, creativity and innovation. But remain aware of the nameless silence.

Silence often holds a deeper power, one that transcends words, thoughts and ideas and resonates within. In the epic Mahabharata, Krishna's role is the ideal epitome of silence--he doesn't wield weapons, yet his presence, wisdom and guidance are the spinal column of Pandavas' strength. His silence symbolizes a eternal truth, the silent yet unwavering force of dharma that supports them.

Lord Krishna's influence in the *Kurukshetra* war goes beyond active participation; it is his counsel, his calm yet powerful silence that ultimately ensures the win of Pandavas. In this way, he represents the eternal silence underlying all sound and action, a reminder that true power often lies not in words or uproar but in a quiet understanding and awareness.

To prevent mental rusting and stagnation, it is essential to cultivate practices that keep the mind engaged in constructive activity and helps in rejuvenation and refreshment of mind. Real power to the mind comes from silencing the mind. Quiet contemplation without words and visualizations calms mental chatter, thereby revealing inner strength.

Subconscious Mind: The Powerhouse within You

Why do few persons succeed and rests fail? Why is someone very rich, and why is someone even struggling for basic requirements of life? Yes, the subconscious mind plays a significant role in shaping success, wealth and other outcomes. Awareness of this part of mind can be transformative. The "awareness factor" makes you more mindful of internal patterns, allowing for better alignment between conscious goals and subconscious programming.

Many people work hard; but they don't get the desired results. It is because they don't focus on one thing with a pure heart and mind. And, also they don't follow the right technique of stirring the subconscious part of their mind. Your efforts yield fruits depending on your faith in you. Your results respond to your mental picture or mental thoughts. Everything is accessible, if you know the subconscious mind; there will be revolution in your life.

Subconscious mind is your unconscious mind which is the powerhouse behind your every move. It regulates your body, actions, breath and even heartbeat. It has the capacity to fulfill your dreams or aspirations. This inner realm holds immense potential. When a dream or desire penetrates the subconscious, it unleashes unstoppable force. Your thoughts, emotions, and actions aligns to make the impossible possible. All you have to do is open your inner eyes.

The subconscious mind shapes your behavior and perception. Acting below the level of conscious awareness, it is the deeper part of your mind that stores beliefs, memories and life experiences, which influence your thoughts, feelings and actions. It operates as a continuous and automatic processor, enabling you to function efficiently. By improving awareness of your thoughts and beliefs, you can cultivate mindset that supports growth and success.

The subconscious mind is like a cloud storage that records every experience, emotion and idea you encounter, storing information that the conscious mind may not immediately recall but which affects you nonetheless. When you learn a skill like riding a bicycle, the memory of balance and pedaling is eventually imprint into your subconscious, so that even decades later, you can do it effortlessly.

This automatic operation shows how your subconscious mind allows you to perform complex tasks without active conscious mind. This lower part of the mind not only remembers facts and processes but also retains emotional memories and core beliefs. Often, these beliefs about yourself, others and the world around you are shaped during early childhood affects your self-image, decision-making power often, without you realizing it.

Your subconscious mind is shaped by programming which comprises repeated thoughts, beliefs and experiences. Positive and negative messages you receive repeatedly from yourself, others or society form a set of subconscious beliefs that influence how you interpret the world. However, the malleability of the subconscious means it can be reprogrammed. Just as negativity may have been ingrained, positive empowering messages can replace them.

~OM~

Chapter 12

Ultimate Use of Mind

The mind is the cradle of creativity, a boundless wellspring from which ideas flows, and shaping dreams into reality. It is the seat of knowledge, where understanding grows and insight bloom, illuminating the path forward. The mind also houses will-power, an inner strength and the courage to pursue one's vision, no matter the obstacles.

The mind and the perfection are not two things, not two existences, but two ways of looking at the same thing, two approaches to the same thing. The ultimate use of mind is possible only when one learns to harness the full potential of the mind. It is far away from the distorted and flickering mind. There are many ways to perfection.

Perfection is not an attainment, but a discovery. It is hidden in every cell of your body. When you practice with your heart and soul, it begins to manifest in your action. Whatsoever you are, you are already perfect in a specific field. Use your mind to know that field which is waiting for you with open arms. Ultimate use of mind means illumine that 'trait' which is hidden.

When you commit to something, give it your full energy and mind. Putting in only partial effort often leads to incomplete or unsatisfactory results. Approach your task with dedication, care and persistence to create long-lasting worthwhile work. In contrast, half-hearted efforts rarely achieve the desired result, leaving things unfinished or lacking quality.

Perfection in any action is the ultimate use of mind. Mastering any specific skill surpasses mediocrity in many. Focus on a single strength gradually blooms into specialization that ensures expertise, efficiency and credibility. Mastery is the pinnacle of mental potential, where intellect, passion and dedication merge. It develops into unparalleled proficiency.

Bhagavad Gita says "**योगः कर्मसु कौशलम्**": Mastery over a skill is often seen as a rare accomplishment, reserved for a select few with seemingly natural talent or extraordinary resources. However, the truth is that anyone with the right mindset, passion in a chosen field, be it marketing, programming, entrepreneurship or any other domain. Robert Greene says: "Expertise is the ultimate form of creativity."

In a world filled with distractions and the allure of endless choices, it's easy to get side-tracked. The temptation to try different things may offer temporary excitement, but it often prevents true progress. While having a broad understanding of various skills can be useful, deep, concentrated focus on a single skill leads to mastery.

When you dedicate yourself to one discipline, you allocate your mental resources effectively, making growth more powerful and efficient. If you dig shallow holes half-heartedly at many places, you may never reach water. But if you dig deep enough in one place, eventually you will strike a wellspring. Mastery requires a similar attitude and approach, pushing boundaries, and continuously refining your abilities within a specific skill.

While many people attempt to be "Jack of all trades," those who focus on one specific area and strive for excellence can achieve a level of expertise and success that transcends the ordinary. Mastery requires commitment, patience, and discipline, but the rewards are substantial. You will not only become highly skilled, but also experience a level of fulfillment and purpose that comes from reaching your full potential.

Ingredients to Master Any Skill

Mastering is a journey from zero proficiency to perfect proficiency. It's easy to improve a little bit a days than trying to become master over a year. Withdraw yourself completely from world and make a wholly attempt to practice a skill every-day without any break. When you practice, feel the divine is also practicing with you.

Mastery over any skill requires consistent, intentional practice, and it's often a process of gradual improvement rather than a series of quick wins. Many people believe that practicing a skill daily will lead to a steady increase in strength or ability. And, while this is true to an extent, it's crucial to recognize that progress is a rarely linear.

If you practice any new skill every-day, you would keep getting better and better and moreover, you will get smarter every-day. Mastery is more like two steps forward and one step back, a series of advances and setbacks that shape a long-term improvement curve. The road to true expertise is slow and often uneven, and there is no shortcut to reach it.

The experience of learning a skill typically involves challenges and obstacles. At times, the practice will feel rewarding as visible progress is made. But then, there will be plateaus, or even regressions, that test one's will power and capacity to fight back from the failures. These are natural phases of the learning process.

During early phases of learning, it can be easy to feel discouraged and question if mastery is even reachable. However, it's in these moments that persistent becomes critical. Every setback or "one step-back" can be viewed as a learning opportunity rather than a failure. If you are repeating the same mistake again and again, you are never going to be able to get there.

Another ingredient of mastery is patience. Many people tend to encourage the idea of "quick fix" or "overnight success", but these are hypothetical. Even those who seem to have achieved mastery with little effort have often put in thousands of hours of hidden practice. Malcolm Gladwell speaks in his book *Outliers*: "If you want to become an expert in any field then for that you will have to practice at least 10,000 hours in it."

Mastery is about commitment over time, where even a few minutes of whole-hearted practice daily can add-up to outstanding progress over months or years. The path to mastery is both rewarding and challenging. The process builds character and goes deeper in your subconscious reinforcing that the destination isn't as important as the path itself.

Each small effort gain accumulates, and each setback makes you stronger. When you approach mastery as a slow, bumpy road, you learn to appreciate the incremental progress, find satisfaction in daily practice, and view challenges as an essential part of growth.

Exploring New Heights

You can be without the mind, but the mind can't be without you. Mind can be destructive if conditioned thoughts and ego-driven desires take you back to feel the freedom and peace in exploring greater depths of awareness. Use the mind not as an end in itself but a pointer to something beyond that looks unattainable from your comfort zone.

Don't be afraid to walk in less-travelled path, to set out on an unknown adventure, to try something new which you had never imagined. Ships are not meant to rest in port, but to cross the horizon into that you can't see. Touching new horizon of experience opens up the senses, brings you back to yourself and effortlessly calms the mind.

The mind is limitless, capable of soaring beyond physical boundaries, exploring the furthest reaches of imagination or understanding the deepest layers of reality. Whether it's chasing dreams, expanding knowledge or diving into inner truths, the direction you choose can shape your experiences and outlook.

You can't reach anywhere until you become the master of your thoughts and decisions. Your thoughts and perspectives have incredible power to determine where you want to go in life. You can go to a wide vast space without looking anywhere. The mind will stop entertaining any thought; and at the end, it will rest on its own roots.

For a spiritual bent of mind, the ultimate use of mind is self-discovery. Your mind, your consciousness, your soul, whatsoever is within you, can be known when the mind turns inwards. Spirituality reveals that all minds are part of one universal mind and all souls are part and parcel of one Supreme. The greatest discovery is discovering oneself.

A spiritual temperament is a spontaneous inclination towards exploring life's deeper mysteries and seeking purpose beyond the physical world that often leads individuals to focus on understanding their true essence. For people with this nature, the mind becomes more than just a tool for navigating daily life; it serves as a bridge to self-realization.

The mind is both the torchbearer and the seeker to a higher understanding of 'Self'. From a spiritual perspective, true essence refers to the changeless, fundamental nature that exists beyond the gross body, subtle body and causal body of your total existence.

This essence is often seen as a pure consciousness that remains a witness of the everyday changes.

For someone with a spiritual temperament, the desire to know this inner essence drives him or her toward practices that help peel back the layers of superficial identity. In this way, the mind becomes the ultimate tool for introspection, guiding one through layers of beliefs, personality and conditioning to reach the core of being.

Through this process, a seeker come to see the mind as a flexible, evolving guide--a companion on a inner journey that ultimately leads back to the timeless and boundless nature of his own being. He recognize that the true essence is not something to be attained or created, it is simply remembered, revealed through quieting of the mind and an opening of the heart.

Achieving Extraordinary Goals

The plan or idea behind achieving extraordinary goals is a motivational note that emphasizes the power of possibility, potential and self-belief which is not a monopoly for a select few; rather anyone with the determination, devotion and strong will-power can realize his or her dream whether it's material, personal or spiritual.

Remember that dreams that seem far-fetched are within your reach. Achieving something unattainable aims is the most refine use of mind--pinnacle of your potential, a testimony to the power of human mind far from the ordinary and inspired by the heroic achievement. To pursue such heights, one must first liberate the mind, allowing it to roam beyond the confines of habit and routine, to wander freely into the realms of possible.

Achieving something 'great' isn't usually a result of luck alone but of consistent effort, commitment and believing in your mind's potential. Each of you has untapped potential, which can be stirred with confidence and a growth mindset. To reach one's fullest potential, the mind must be freed from limitations, only then can it shift into the depths of the subconscious, where hidden dreams reside, cloaked in silence, waiting to be manifested.

Each of you carries within an un-sprouted dream, an unspoken dream woven into the layers of your subconscious. It could be the bubble of a dry-out passion, a vision of an achievement that seemed too vast to articulate, or a purpose that has murmured to you but has yet to be heard. This dream, untainted by external expectations, lies neglected by the conventions of everyday life. To let it sprout requires introspection and courage.

It demands a moment of stillness, a willingness to close one's eyes and explore the inner world asking: "What truly moves me?" "What unfulfilled vision stirs within?" Once the un-manifested dream starts breathing, it is not enough to simply acknowledge it. To realize such a vision, one must engage whole-heartedly in the pursuit of this goal, leaving no stone unturned.

Many people struggle to believe in their capabilities. This is not a path for the chicken-hearted; it requires relentless determination and a willingness to overcome obstacles, however inaccessible they may seem. In this quest, every challenge becomes a stepping-stone, every setback a lesson, and every victory a reminder of why the journey is worth the effort.

To manifest a dream is to become the architect of one's destiny, to build a reality out of a vision born from the depths of the mind. Achieving an extraordinary goal is not merely about individual success or achievement. It is about the journey of ultimate use of mind and transformation. This pursuit is the excellent use of mind--a tribute to the boundless potential of human thought, where every moment becomes an opportunity to transcend, to create, and to fulfill that long-hidden dream.

Develop Pure Attentiveness

Attention is a state of silent, unwavering awareness, free from the noise of piercing thoughts. Instead of actively thinking, you allow thoughts to pass through, as if they happen on their own effortlessly. Look at someone or something without forming judgments or inner chatting--just being fully present, purely observant. In this calm alertness, you become an observer of your mind, connecting more deeply to the moment, experiencing life directly and unfiltered.

Just as the weather changes, so do your feelings. Your mind has many (apparent and hidden) layers and moods are just one part. When you use your mind to be fully attentive, you unlock a deeper level of awareness. This helps you connect more honestly with others, make better decisions, and live with a sense of inner peace. Instead of being swept away by temporary emotions, you can remain centered and experiencing life in its true form.

It is the ability to see things clearly, without the lens of personal judgments, biases and emotional reactions. When you practice pure attentiveness, you will be aware of waves of anger, fear, lust, jealousy etc erupting in your inner ocean of consciousness. Take this feeling as temporary, where you can see it as just one moment in a larger spectrum of experiences.

Attentiveness helps you step-back from the vortex of emotions and gain a broader view of life. This approach allows you to respond more thoughtfully rather than reacting mechanically. When you are attentive, you create space in your mind. It allows you to choose your responses rather than simply reacting based on mood.

For instance, if someone says something hurtful, your immediate reaction might be anger or hurt. But with attentiveness, you can pause and see the situation as it is. You might realize that the other's persons word reflect their mood or struggles. By staying present and observant, you can choose to respond with wisdom rather than anger.

The purpose of cultivating attentiveness is to live a balanced life, where you are not constantly tossed around by your moods. This doesn't mean you can ignore your emotions; rather, you acknowledge them without letting them take over. Attentiveness is about seeing things as they are, without distortion. It allows you to experience life fully while staying grounded.

Infinite Possibilities within You

If you focus on failure; failure is bound to happen. Conversely, if you focus on success; you will realize your ream. A mind focused on others' opinion, validation or expectations can't be a gateway to success. Choose thoughts that empower your will-power and reject that drains your energy. Discern what serves your growth and dismiss negativity.

There are infinite possibilities within you; you have same strength of capabilities. Find what hidden potential within you is ready to emerge out; otherwise you have to remain dependent on others. Focus inward, cultivate self-belief and unlock your true potential for success and fulfillment. Mind is a potent mechanism that shapes the outcome of your life.

Mind operates as a window, choosing to either accept or reject experiences, thoughts and beliefs. This process of mental filtering becomes especially significant when pursuing success in any specific field. Without the proper training of the mind, it is nearly impossible to reach the zenith of success. Activate the full potential of your intelligence (*buddhi*).

In simple words, when you learn to direct your thoughts and energy effectively, you unlock the dormant power of the mind and set yourself on the path towards reward and honor. Concentration is a key aspect of mental discipline, yet it is also one of the most challenging skills to master. Otherwise, distractions scatter your thoughts and dilute your efforts.

The dispersion of mind—the tendency to allow thoughts and focus to roam aimlessly—is a apparent obstacle to success. When your mind is turbulent and disturbed, your thoughts become chaotic and directionless, weakening your ability to perform at your best. Conversely, a well-trained mind focused on solo target, leads you to powerful and efficient action.

The mind's ability to permit or reject ideas is not passive, it is an active choice influenced by your thoughts, beliefs and attitudes. By consciously choosing which ideas, emotions and goals to nurture, you create mental patterns that align with success. This alignment helps you to develop what can be described as a success mindset.

When your intelligence is directed by a focused mind, it becomes sharp and purposeful, creating an inner alignment empowers you to overcome challenges, remain balance in the face of setbacks, and maintain a positive outlook. Intelligence is the engine that drives your success, but the mind is the wheel that steers you in the right direction.

Stupendous success requires a degree of mental dedication and depth of focus that surpasses the ordinary. Those who succeed in exemplary ways are often those who train their minds to think beyond limitations. They are able to imagine possibilities, embrace challenges and persist in all even and odd situations.

Connecting Mind to Cosmic Energy

Mind is a connecting junction between you and the cosmic energy. It is a link between the limited and the unlimited dimension of existence. It bridges two quite opposite things—microscopic and macroscopic. If your physical existence is watched from the cosmic lens, you are no more than microscopic creature.

But you are simply not just the body. Unless one realizes this truth, one will remain in misery, anguish and suffering.

You are not a just a physical body with mind, intelligence and consciousness. You are made-up of energy and exist in an infinite space where everything is vibrating energy. You are both transmitter and receiver of energy. One of the biggest challenges for you is crossing over the physical world of limitations. Your mind is simply a wave; the cosmic energy is the ocean. You need to understand the symbiosis between individual mind and the cosmic energy.

Worldly temptations, which include desires, dreams and lust, are distractions that can stop you to connect with cosmic energy. These temptations often create a sense of separation between your innate energy and the rest of existence. It gives you an illusion of individuality and isolation, which leads to suffering and perpetuates the cycling of longing and dissatisfaction.

Your mind is victim of inescapable duality of nature, while this cosmic or universal energy is the force that underpins the whole existence, an infinite resource of vitality and insight that binds all things together in a geometric way. By connecting one's mind to an unlimited supply of cosmic energy, one can transcend the limitations of defined world, disconnection with material attachments and finding a path toward unity and spiritual liberation.

Your mind has the capacity to send and receive energy anywhere and at any time. One of the daunting tasks for you is to understand how to live as an energy being in a world where everything is made up of energy. Every thought your mind generate and every word you speak from the simplest task of breathing, walking and eating to the web of your emotions and feelings needs energy as the vehicle needs fuel to move.

An irresistible power of the mind is to connect effortlessly from unseen creature to gigantic star. It does things that you have never thought it can do. The individual energy field and the universal is essentially the same. These complex thoughts or emotions, whether constructive or destructive, carry their own energetic vibrations than can shape your experiences and have an impact on the cosmic energy ever-vibrating on its own.

~OM~

Chapter 13

Mind: Tool for Divinity

Generally, your mind remains engrossed in mundane activities through five senses of see, hear, feel, taste and smell. This external experience, known as the world of *Maya* or illusion, can be deceiving. *Maya* is the illusion that eclipses the ultimate truth, eternal nature of existence, making you see things as separate, changing and impermanent.

Think of it like a movie screen. When you watch a film, you see distinct characters, actions and emotional drama unfolding. However, you know that these characters and scenes are unreal—they are simply images projected onto the silver screen. *Maya* works in a similar way, tricking your mind into thinking that what you perceive is all there is to life.

But, like the movie, screen behind the images, there is underpinning deeper reality behind everything you experience; one is stable, unchanging and eternal. In the spiritual realm, the world of illusions includes all the things that change and eventually fades away: your physical body (of five elements), your relationships, your possessions and even thoughts and emotions.

Since everything you sense and feel changes, your mind is constantly moving from one thing to the next, searching for satisfaction, joy or meanings in life that can't be termed as permanently. The problem is that these flux-like experiences keep your attention outwardly focused, drawing your mind away from the peace and bliss that lies within.

But if you allow the mind to turn inwards instead, you may begin to sense a different reality. Through practices like self-absorption, intensive contemplation or simply being awareness, you start to recognize a part of your being that is steady and peaceful—a space beyond thoughts, emotions and fluctuations of the outer world.

This inward focus is often called the practice of "touching the divine within." It leads you away from illusion and toward the true essence of your existence; an esoteric experience that awakened yogis and highly spiritual saints call "*chidanand*" means pure consciousness and bliss. It is the blissful consciousness is said to be true nature of every embodied soul.

चिदानंद रुप: शिवोहम शिवोहम ||

Unlike the fleeting happiness you seek from external things, this inner bliss doesn't rely on anything outside yourself. It's steady and present, even if you aren't always aware of it. In a way, you could compare *chidanand* to the cloudless sky where everything is transparent and crystal clear. Clouds come and go, but sky remains calm and undisturbed.

Similarly, beneath the turbulent and tearing thoughts of your mind, there is a state of pure, calm awareness. When you turn your focus inward by curtailing all senses, the mind can stat to taste or experience this blissful consciousness. This is a process that demands constant practice, patience as the mind gradually starts loosening the strings of attachments to temporary things.

Through this inward exploration, you begin to see that life is more than passing scenes on the surface. Even though your senses show you an outer world of change, the awareness within you is beyond time and space realm. This awareness is the divine essence, the ultimate truth that *Maya* or illusion has hidden from you.

धूमेनाव्रियते वह्निर्यथाऽऽदर्शों मलेन च।
यथोल्बेनावृतो गर्भस्तथा तेनेदमावृतम्।।भगवद्गीता, 3.38।।

As a fire is enveloped by smoke, as a mirror by dust and as an embryo by the membrane, so is the divine essence, the ultimate truth of a human covered by this desire. Sri Krishna teaches the mode of this envelopement.

Living with your true nature is freeing yourself from the clutches of illusion or Maya. You may still go through daily challenges of life, but the mind rooted in *chidanand*, becomes less affected by them. As you grow in this awareness, you come closer to experiencing life in its full-flowering, living with compassion, peace and joy that flow from within.

Begin with Mind & Body

Right now, your whole experience is related to mind or body or both. The mind and body are existential truths of your existence, and you often spend your life exploring their challenges, desires and instincts. However, divinity remains an elusive concept, often perceived as an external notion or a distant idea rather than a present reality.

It all happens because your inner divinity, like the reflection of the moon on a disturbed lake, is clouded by layers of emotional and mental imbalances. Imagine a serene lake at night, its surface calm a reflective, mirroring the full-moon's light in full splendor. In such a state, the lake offers a clear reflection, symbolizing the purity and clarity of one's inner 'Self' or divine.

But when layers of disturbance in forms of ripples, waves and mud disrupt its surface, the reflection becomes distorted or even vanishes. In the same way, when you allow layers of anger, hatred and lust and other tearing emotions to disturb your mind, they act like the debris on the lake, obscuring your ability to perceive your own divinity.

Anger, for instance, has a potent energy that can consume your thoughts and actions, distorting your true nature. Hatred further blinds you, pulling you into cycles of resentment and hostility. Lust and worthless desires similarly tie you to external pursuits, keeping your focus on immediate gratification rather than deeper, lasting peace.

These emotions and impulses are not inherently "bad", rather, it is their unchecked nature and overwhelming influence that casts a veil over your inner self. Peeling away these layers requires self-awareness, a deeper commitment to inner growth. By learning to observe these emotions with letting them to control you, you begin to calm the lake of your mind.

The world is less than real. The divine is always empirically un-manifest. Trained the mind to exclude the unreal and focus on the real. Everything is full of misery (*sarvam dukham*), no matter how it looks appealing and appeasing to the senses from the surface level. One should withdraw the mind from the pleasures of ever-changing world.

Whatsoever you are, accept yourself. You are part of the eternal, the unmoved and silent witness of your inner moods. Many spiritual practices help you dissolve anger and hatred, while detachment and moderation can control lust and desires. Gradually, the lake of the mind becomes clearer, allowing the moon--a symbol of inner divinity--to shine through.

Your mindset shapes your world. So, it has been said that there are as many worlds as minds. Break the mental barriers to experience 'Ultimate'. Divine is "*nirvikar*" (unperturbed, unaffected) and "*sampurna*" (free from any emotions and any desires). It is a state of calmness, and detachment, where one is not influenced by external factors or internal emotions.

This process of uncovering divinity is not about reaching somewhere to unknown dimension; it's about returning to the innate purity and peace that already reside within everyone of human being. In calming the turbulent waters of the mind, you rediscover your essence that is free from illusion and inundated with compassion, wisdom and bliss.

Understand the Patterns of Ordinary Mind

Change is the law of nature. Everything changes, and so is your mind. You move as a crowd, and you think as a crowd. Everyone is 'unconscious' about the inner divinity that dwells in every human-being. Only the awakened yogis remain aware of their witnessing consciousness. Intuitive awareness alone can give you the experience of 'divine' within you.

The world and your mind have become one. So, mind wants more and more. The mind doesn't yearn what is in your possession, but rather which is far away. It refers to human tendency to undervalue what you have and idealize what you don't. The mind is often driven by desire, which creates an illusion that satisfaction lies in the objects or things beyond your reach.

Perpetual desire of the mind is to seek novelty, freshness and variety. This creates a cycle where once you attain something, the novelty fades and the mind shifts its focus to something else--always something that feels elusive or distant. This pattern, which often, leaves you feeling unfulfilled, is something called "grass always looks greener on the neighbors side."

In essence, it describes how the mind constantly craves new experiences (*navam, navam*), ideas and sensations. Rather than being content with what is, the mind tends to move from one thought, object or experience to another, always seeking something different and unfamiliar. This tendency can lead to restlessness, as mind seldom rests before moving on to the next.

By recognizing and understanding this tendency, one can cultivate deeper inner peace, by learning to appreciate and focus on the present moment, instead of being driven by the never ending search for novelty. To transcend the mind, you have to cultivate a state of awareness beyond inner chatting, reaching a place of silence and clarity.

A silently pure and ripple-less mind is pure mind. It happens in deep sleep when there remains no desire or no seeking in mind, but you are not aware during those moments. You must be aware in waking state too that allows individuals to transcend the talkative mind that creates a false sense of egoistic self and separates you from your true nature.

- Mind is a mere illusion
- Deeper body is mind
- Pure mind is present moment
- Turn closer to your essence
- Recognize your divine center

Still Mind: Doorway to Divine

You identify yourself with mind. Human emotions, such as happiness and sadness, provide an example of how the divine may be present but not always perceptible. When you say: "I am happy" or "I am sad", you are expressing the state of your mind. These emotions are real and intensely felt, yet they are intangible--they cannot be held, seen or touched.

The mind, the source of these emotions, undoubtedly exists, yet it is not something you can directly perceive. This experience of your mind offers a subtle parallel to your experience of the divine:

both are intangible yet impactful; hidden yet influential. Behind mind, the divine serves as a hidden source of strength, energy and inspiration.

While the mind stirs thoughts, feelings and perceptions, it functions within a framework that the divine empowers. No thought can exists without mind. Similarly, no mind or intelligence or embodied consciousness can exist without divine. Without this ultimate life-force, the mind itself would have no energy or capacity to operate.

One can easily be aware of his/her mind by thoughts, feelings and emotions. But it's not easy to connect with something deeper often called the "divine soul" or "pure consciousness". Being unimaginable and inexpressible; the divine is beyond human's mind and intelligence. It's an all-encompassing truth that can't be fully grasped or articulated.

It is like an intangible, unseen presence of clarified butter (*ghee*) in milk. It is present within milk, but it is not directly visible or accessible; as it requires a deliberate, skilled process of churning to be extracted. Similarly, the divine presence pervades everything, though you can't perceive it directly, you can only contemplate its presence through an inner churning process.

This churning process comprises inner reflection, self-inquiry and subtle awareness. Spiritual practices, much like the churning of milk, helps you extract a deeper truth that is already within you but often concealed by dust of ego, desires and distractions. It is through this churning that you get a glimpse of the divine, something deeper than your mind, intelligence and lower self.

In this way, the divine could be seen as the underpinning force or pure consciousness that activates the mind. This spiritual truth reveals how divine supports mental and emotional functions without being directly visible. The expansion of the mind, in this context, becomes a journey towards a deeper awareness of the divine.

To expand the mind doesn't convey to merely accumulate worldly knowledge or information or acquire new skills; rather, it suggests a deeper opening—a readiness to receive, to intuit, and to go beyond conditional thought. The divine, in this expanded awareness of mind, becomes not just an idea or notion but an intimate, ever-present reality.

To connect with this deeper essence, the activity of the mind needs to be standstill. When train of thoughts stop, the true essence or the divine "within", can start to emerge and be felt. When the mind is quiet, you become aware of the deeper and divine part of yourself. The silent mind holds boundless peace, and you become receptive vessel for the divine.

The mind is dwelling place for desires, anxieties and dualities much like Mathura, a place that witnessed Krishna's earliest trials. And the divine is like *Vrindavan*, it reflects a pure state of being, untouched by mental conflicts and overflowing with love, peace and eternal joy. The entire spiritual journey begins in Mathura; and culminates in *Vrindavan*.

How to Regained Pure Mind?

The original mind is pure without any modifications (*vrittis*). The essence of every mind is inherently pure, untouched and divine. However, as individuals traverse through the cycles of life and rebirth, the mind loses its purity and becomes contaminated by layers of accumulated impressions, desires, fears and attachments.

These layers metaphorically referred to as "dust", veil the original mind, causing one to feel separate from the divine self, which is inherently perfect and limitless. The mind is often compared to a base metal, like iron or lead—common, unrefined and burdened with impurities. However, through devotion and surrender to the divine, it can undergo a transformation similar to the alchemical process, turning it into something precious like gold.

The original mind, in its true form, is not distinct from the divine 'Self'. It is free from ego, desires, and the illusions of the material world. It is a state of being where one exists in complete harmony with the universal consciousness, experiencing a sense of peace, love and unity. However, the journey through countless lifetimes—filled with experiences, choices and karmic consequences—clouds this purity.

The ego grows stronger, attachments deepen, and the mind becomes entangled in the web of duality, perceiving a separation between oneself and the divine. Yet, this obscured state is not ever-lasting. Spiritual preaching reminds you that it is possible to rediscover and reconnect with the original mind. This process, however, requires conscious effort, devotion and surrender.

Devotion, or *bhakti*, is the act of surrendering oneself to a higher power, a divine force, or the ultimate truth. It involves cultivating a deep sense of love, trust and reverence toward the divine. Through devotion, one transcends the limitations of the ego and begins to see beyond the mirage of the material world. The divine, in turn, becomes a mirror, reflecting the purity that already exists within. The final wording of *Bhagavad Gita* says:

सर्वधर्मान्परित्यज्य मामेकं शरणं व्रज।
अहं त्वा सर्वपापेभ्यो मोक्षयिष्यामि मा शुचः।।18.66।।

Abandoning all duties, take refuge in Me alone: I will liberate thee from all sins; grieve not.

Surrender, or *sharanagati*, is another key aspect of this inward exploration. It involves rising high above the illusion of control and trusting the divine plan. Surrender doesn't imply weakness or passivity; rather, it is a conscious choice to release the burdens of fear, doubt, and resistance. By surrendering, one acknowledges the limitations of the ego and aligns with the infinite wisdom of the divine. It allows the accumulated dust on the mind to be cleared, revealing the original, unblemished state of being.

The process of regaining the pure mind is deeply transformative. It often requires regular spiritual practices such as mantra recitation, pilgrimage, prayer, selfless service and meditation. It helps in stilling the mind, and experience your true nature. Prayer deepens a connection with the divine, nurturing a sense of intimacy and guidance. Selfless service shifts the focus from self-centeredness to compassion and generosity, dissolving the ego's grip.

Each of these practices acts as a tool to cleanse the mind, peeling back the layers of illusion and revealing the divine essence within. Ultimately, the journey toward reclaiming the pure mind is not about becoming something new; it is about returning to what one has always been. It is about rediscovering the inherent divinity that lies at the core of every being.

इन्द्रियाणिपराण्याहुरिन्द्रियेभ्यःपरंमनः।
मनसस्तुपराबुद्धिर्योबुद्धेःपरतस्तुसः॥भगवद्गीता, 3.42।।

When compared with the physical body which is gross, external and limited, the senses are certainly superior as they are more subtle, internal and have a wider range of activity. The mind is superior to the senses, as the senses cannot do anything independently without the help of the mind. The mind can perform the functions of the five senses. The intellect is superior to the mind because it is endowed with the faculty of discrimination. When the mind is in a state of doubt, the intellect comes to its resuce. The Self, the Witness, is superior even to the intellect, as the intellect borrows its light from the Self.

Sense organs, Mind and intellect are the three check points for human body like the three governing body of a nation or a system. Sense organs are like "*karyapalika*" refers to the executive branch (which enforces laws), Mind is like "*vidhayika*" to the legislative branch (which makes laws), and intellect is like "*nyaypalika*" to the judicial branch (which interprets laws).

Ascend or Descend of Consciousness: Both Possibilities

Man can 'rise' by higher awareness and insight; or 'fall' by ego-driven thoughts and ignorance in consciousness realm. Man is neither animal nor awakened ones. In contrast, human beings stand at a crossroads, torn between higher and lower realm of consciousness. One leads upward toward growth, wisdom and self-realization, while the other descends into ignorance and despair. You can be aware only when you know where you stand between the two.

In the complexity of varied life, the journey of a bud transforming into a flower or a tadpole metamorphosing into a frog unfolds as a pre-destined path. Their existence is programmed by the laws of nature, where each stage of growth is an unavoidable progression. Humans, however, stand apart in the grand design of creation. Unlike other beings, human possess a natural gift free will and the capacity for self-awareness.

This distinct endowment places humanity at a crossroads, where the latent for enlightenment and liberation exists alongside the possibility of regression to lower states of consciousness. The journey of human life is not merely biological but spiritual and existential too. A bud has no choice but to bloom, and a tadpole but predictably evolve into a frog.

Humans, however, can transcend their biological and instinctual limitations. The potential for enlightenment is a possibility uniquely accessible to humans. This potential is not pre-determined; it must be cultivated consciously through effort, reflection and discipline. In Buddhism, enlightenment is referred to as '*nirvana*".

However, the path to "*nirvana*" is fraught with challenges. Human beings are endowed not only with the potential for transcendence but also with vulnerabilities that can lead them to fall. Greed, anger, ignorance and attachment are powerful forces that can cloud judgment and pull individuals away from their higher purpose.

When humans succumb to these negative tendencies, they risk dissolving into states of lower consciousness. For example, a person who lives consumed by greed, lust and selfishness may act in ways that harm others, creating negative acts (*karma*) that perpetuates their suffering. Similarly, unchecked anger or ignorance can lead to actions that degrade one's character.

The division between humans and other creatures lies in the power of choice. While nature directs the bud to bloom and the tadpole to grow, humans must consciously decide whether to ascend or descend on the level of consciousness. This choice requires awareness, discipline and effort. To born as human is not end of life; one must expand his mind to its highest potential.

Lower creatures live in accord with nature, their basic needs of life met effortlessly. They are content, driven by instinct, free from complexities of ambition or desire. Enlightened beings, having transcended worldly illusions experience fulfillment, peace and liberation. They have reached the pinnacle of their journey, free from the struggles of choice and conflict.

In contrast, human beings stand at a crossroads, torn between two paths or choices. One leads upward, toward growth, wisdom and self-realization, while other descends into ignorance and darkness. Ultimately, the human journey is a testament to the incredible power of free will and self-decision. The capacity for enlightenment or divinity is a insightful gift, but it is not guaranteed. It must be earned through 'low living and high thinking' approach to life.

~OM~

Chapter 14

Beyond Mind

You are neither body nor mind. You are beyond both. In essence, you are pure consciousness, ultimate reality and "Self". This is your innate consciousness, the core of your existence which is present in all times, places and circumstances. Even in deep sleep, when you forget your mind-body identification, your true essence remains with you. It is your subjective experience or universal "I" which in contracted form becomes empirical mind (ego).

This is the transcendental and formless essence of your being. Self-inquiry is the doorway to reach beyond mind. In *Vedantic* philosophy, this concept is often explored through the practice of *neti, neti*, meaning "not this, not this." It helps you transcend identification with limited aspects of your existence, such as mind, body or intellect. To realize your true nature, you move inwards by curtailing mind, body and senses, which is beyond all conceptual boundaries.

Observing the Mind

One of the basic insights of *neti-neti* is that you can observe your thoughts; emotions and mental fluctuations like you watch any object. For example, when a wave of thought rises in the surface layer of your mind, there is an awareness that perceives it. Similarly, when an emotion such as love or hate manifests, you recognize its presence.

This ability to witness mental activity implies that you are not the mind itself, but something subtler and more extensive. The observer--the awareness--is distinct from the observed. This realization begins the process of separating the self from identification with transient mental states.

Beyond the Body

The body is often the first layer of identity you associate with the self. Yet, *neti-neti* invites you to ask: Is the body truly me? The body changes constantly --cells regenerate, appearances alter and physical sensations come and go. If you can observe these changes, you cannot be identical to them. Like the mind, the body becomes an object of awareness, not the subject. Through this inquiry, the seeker realizes that the body is merely an instrument, a vehicle for experience, but not the essence of who you are.

Beyond Intelligence

The intellect, or the faculty of reasoning and analysis, is another common point of identification. However, even intelligence can be observed. For example, when solving a problem or analyzing a concept, there is a deeper awareness witnessing the intellectual process. The intellect, too, is subject to fluctuation--it sharpens, dulls, and evolves over time.

Self-inquiry is a divine journey from unconsciousness to consciousness. The limitations in mind and intelligence have veiled your true nature. By observing its limitations, you comes to know that intelligence, like the mind and body, is not the ultimate self but a tool used for self-realization. Divine truth is revealed when you gather yourself totally at one point.

The Ultimate Reality

Having negated identification with the body, mind and intellect, what remains? The practice of self-inquiry guides you toward the recognition of your true nature as pure consciousness. This pure consciousness is often described in Vedanta as *Sat-Chit-Ananda*—existence, consciousness and bliss. It is unchanging, eternal, and self-luminous untouched by the fluctuations of the material world.

Realizing that you are not the body, mind or intellect doesn't mean rejecting or ignoring them. Instead, it allows you to engage with these facets of existence from a place of freedom and non-attachment. You understand that while these instruments are vital for navigating the world, they don't define your essence. This shift in perspective dissolves fear, attachment, and suffering, as you no longer fault the impermanent for the eternal.

Most of you have assumed a sense of individual consciousness, identifying solely with your peculiar traits. You see a world of many dissimilar waves that seems separate from you. In reality, the entire universe is nothing but one un-differentiated reality, and that everything is that supreme consciousness expressed in different forms.

State of Pure Awareness

The mind is the world that you are familiar with. It projects the external reality through five senses and intelligence. Everything you experience, interpret, or imagine originates from the mind's innate capacity to organize and relate to the perceiving world around you. However, the mind also has a tendency to drift towards the gross, manifested world, latching onto objects, ideas or stimuli to sustain its activity.

This inclination to seek external support keeps the mind in constant motion, creating a cycle of attachment, distraction and identification with the tangible world. To reach beyond the mind is to move beyond its dependency on forms, objects and concepts. It requires cultivating an awareness that is free from the limitations of identification and attachment. In breath meditation, practitioner focus on the gap between incoming and outgoing breath.

The mind, in its essence, cannot move without a focal point or support. Whether it be the resonance of words, the vibration of sound, or the image of an object, the mind requires something to cling its attention. This dependency on external or internal stimuli creates a ceaseless flow of thoughts, emotions, and sensations. This whole process hides your true nature. Yet, the key to transcending the mind lies not in suppressing its activity but in understanding and working with its nature.

A technique for transcending the mind is to dissolve awareness in the space between two consecutive thoughts. In your daily life, thoughts arise and subside in rapid succession, creating the illusion of a continuous mental stream. However, there remains always the gap between two rapid thoughts, untouched by the mental activity. By reposing awareness in this gap, one can transcend the mind and have a glimpse of infinite stillness that underlies all thoughts.

Similarly, the silence between two musical notes holds a portal to transcendence. Music, often described as traditional method of meditation in eastern world, can serve as a powerful medium to move beyond the mind. The soothing musical notes captives your attention. Yet, it is in the silence between these notes where a deeper stillness resides. This silence can carry your awareness in the divine dimension where sound and silence merge.

To transcend the mind is not to escape it, but to recognize its nature as a launching-pad rather than the essence of your being. The path beyond the mind begins with observing the subtle spaces of silence and gaps, using them as getaways to the infinite awareness that lies within. It is in this journey that one truly understands the deeper truth that transcends all thoughts.

Path of Wisdom: Going Beyond Mind

The mind is inclined towards worldly activities that solidify the ego, creating a false sense of identity and separation. This attachment to the ego blinds one to the deeper truth of existence. To transcend the mind is to detach from its ego-driven tendencies and align with the higher Self. Beyond the mind lie peace, unity and the boundless potential of the higher Self.

To understand the path of wisdom, one must dive deeper into the nature of the mind, the role of intelligence and the higher self. Mind continuously generates thoughts, desires and intentions. These intentions often arise from past experiences, conditioning and external stimuli. The mind, like a restless ocean, creates waves of thoughts.

These thought patterns, while seemingly integral to your identity, are not the essence of who you truly are. Intelligence acts as a discerning faculty. It evaluates the intentions that arise in your mind, accepting or rejecting them based on reason, logic or ethical considerations. Intelligence functions as a tool to navigate life, helping to make decisions and solve problems.

However, intelligence itself is not the ultimate authority. It, too, is a construct connected to the physical and mental realms, influenced by the ego and the societal norms. You are neither the mind nor the intelligence; but the silent witness—the observer who remains unaffected by the appearing and disappearing of thoughts and judgments.

This silent witness, often referred to as pure consciousness or awareness, is the essence of your being. It is unchanging, eternal, and unmoved by the fluctuations of the mind or the biases of the intelligence. Recognizing yourself as this witness is a pivotal step in spiritual growth.

Going beyond the mind is the path of wisdom. This process involves dis-identifying from the non-stop chatter of the mind and the ego's compulsive need for validation and control. The mind is a valuable servant but a poor master. When one is entangled in the mind's narratives, it leads to suffering, confusion and a sense of separation from the higher self.

Wisdom emerges when one steps back and observes the mind without attachment, understanding that its activity is not the ultimate reality. Pure knowledge, the hallmark of the higher self, transcends the dualities of right and wrong, good and bad. This knowledge is not borrowed or bookish; it is an experiential understanding of one's true nature.

It is the realization that you are part of an infinite, interconnected whole. This higher self is not driven by the ego, which thrives on separation, comparison and self-interest. Instead, it operates from a place of unity, love and compassion. To access this higher 'Self', one must develop practices that silences the mind and sharpens your awareness.

Beyond the Play of Thoughts

The world is often mistaken as a carefree playground where one can play with thoughts, emotions without caution, but in harsh reality, it is more like a marshy land fraught with uncertainty and hidden perils. When the mind is at play, the reality which is within the mind or which is beyond the mind will not manifest itself.

In a playground, mistakes are accepted and the environment encourages standing up again and again in spite of repeated falls down without fear of drastic consequences. In contrast, the treacherous terrain of the world demands awareness, balance and prudence to avoid slipping into pitfalls that can hinder progress or cause harm.

Life's challenges, in any form, are rarely straightforward. Temptations, deceit, and unforeseen adversities often lurk beneath the soft-appearing surface, ready to destabilize even the most experienced traveler. A single misstep can lead to significant setbacks, emphasizing the importance of resilience, adaptability and careful decision-making.

An ennui-stricken mind, weighed down by monotony, often turns to the pleasure of the senses in a desperate bid for novelty. Ennui, a strange existential boredom, creates a void in your heart that demands stimulation to escape its oppressive grip. The senses—sight, sound, taste, touch and smell—offer a fleeting respite. It can momentarily awaken a dull spirit.

However, this pursuit of pleasure is fleeting and often cyclical, as the relief offered by sensory indulgence dissipates, leaving the mind yearning for more meaningful fulfillment. The mind tied to senses serve as both refuge and trap, offering distraction but rarely satiating deeper needs. Reality is stillness. Mental modifications must come to an end.

The problem is the distortion set-up by the mind. Solution must be calming the thought generating mind down. Silencing the mind is not something a novice seeker of truth can do. It slows down on its own, like a spinning top eventually comes to rest. When the players (thoughts) stop playing in the playground (of mind), the reality manifests.

Beyond the play of thoughts dwells higher state of awareness (beyond the limitations of thought, ego and sensory experience). This inward movement leads to the supreme bliss often mentioned as the state of "*Chidanand*"—a confluence of pure consciousness (*chit*) and bliss (*ananda*). Here, you don't exist as an individual. Sense of separation disappears.

It is a state where the individual realizes his/her true nature free from the illusions and distractions of the disturbed mind. The *Chidananda* state is not an external destination but a return to one's inherent nature. It is a state of being where duality dissolves, and the individual experience unity. This state is marked by nameless and effortless bliss, not derived from external dependencies but emanating from the realization of one's oneness with the whole.

In this state, the division between subject and object, doer and deed dissolves. Life flows spontaneously, guided by the intelligence of the infinite. It doesn't mean the annihilation of the mind, but dropping of all thoughts. It is conscious stilling of the thoughts and stop the mind from playing. It brings freedom, unshakable peace and boundless love. It is awakening to the eternal *sat-chit-ananda* (existence, consciousness, bliss) that has always been present. It is the realization that the door to divine bliss has never been closed, one simply needed to step through by turning inward and embracing the infinite.

~OM~

Chapter 15

Conclusions

To know the mind through the mind is like trying to see your own eyes without a mirror. It is a perplexing pursuit as the very tool for observation is also the object being observed. To connect with native readers and resonate deeply with their cultural heritage, the author has skillfully woven quotes from renowned authors and *slokas* from classical scriptures. It allows readers to see the continuity of human thought and the universal quest for knowing the human mind.

This book titled "I Know the Human Mind" begins with an insightful introduction to the human mind, offering a foundational understanding of its intricate workings. It seamlessly bridges the gap between the scientific inquiry and spiritual exploration, presenting the mind as a dynamic entity that straddles both realms.

By doing so, the introduction lays the groundwork for a holistic exploration of the mind, encouraging readers to appreciate its complexity from multiple perspectives. The following chapters delve into a critical distinction: the difference between the mind and the brain. In clear language, the author demystifies this often-confusing relationship, explaining how the brain functions as the tangible, physical organ that governs neurological processes, while the mind represents the intangible domain of thoughts, emotions and consciousness.

This lucid explanation equips readers with a framework to navigate the nuances of these two interconnected yet distinct entities. Building on this foundation, the subsequent chapters takes a deeper dive into the relationship between the mind and consequences. Here, the book explores how the mind acts as a bridge to consciousness, enabling self-awareness, perception and the experience of being.

Individual mind vs. collective mind (chapter 5) represents two interconnected but distinct levels of human thought and consciousness. Individuals contribute to and are influenced by the collective mind, whether through participation in cultural activities, adherence to societal norms, or the acceptance of shared knowledge. Individual mind can challenge and transform the collective mind as it emerges from collective thoughts, values and knowledge of individuals.

The heart of the book lies in the captivating chapters on how the mind works. These sections unravel the mechanisms through which the mind processes information, forms memories and shapes perception of reality. By blending engaging examples with cutting-edge research, the author brings to life the fascinating ways the mind operates, offering readers both enlightenment and practical insights.

There are as many worlds as minds. Our minds filter and interpret the world uniquely. For example, the same event can evoke joy in one person and sadness in another, depending on their past experiences and emotional state. The chapter "Types of Mind" underscores the infinite variety of individual perception, reminding you to celebrate human differences and strive for understanding amidst this diversity.

No thoughts or no mind is not a state. It is the reality on which thoughts appear. This is the essence of chapter 7 (No-mind State). It emphasizes transcending flickering mind to achieve pure presence and awareness. By silencer mental chatter, one accesses a deeper state of being, free from judgment, ego and distraction.

The "psychology of mind" explores the nature of thought and its influence on perception, emotions and reality. It is study human behavior in a joint collaboration of neuroscience, sociology and traditional Indian philosophy. It highlights how the mind shapes experiences through conditioned thinking and beliefs.

The chapter "evolution of mind" is both captivating and thought-provoking, tracing the development of cognitive practices in human through the ages. It delves into the growth of intellectual, emotional, and spiritual capacities, unveiling how our thoughts, creativity, and awareness have shaped civilizations.

Although, anatomically modern humans have existed for around 300,000 years, the mental capacities, cognitive skills and behaviors of early Homo sapiens differ significantly from those of modern humans. Earlier, man used to live in small, tight-knit groups and their survival depended on cooperation. While brain size hasn't changed much, the structure and functionality of the brain have evolved.

The psychology of mind is amazing, but it is questionable, if mind is blessing or a curse, a devil or an angel. The scientific study of mental processes, emotions and thoughts has taken long strides during the last century. The psychology of mind (chapter 8) is study human behavior that explores the workings of human thought processes, including perception, memory, emotions, reasoning and decision-making.

Early humans had less specialized brains compared to different patterns of cortical folding and neural connectivity. Chapter 9

(Evolution of mind) refers to the development of cognitive practices in human. This process is closely linked to biological evolution, where natural selection favored traits that improved survival and reproduction.

Learning to cultivate and balance your thoughts is the foundation for living a life rich in purpose and meaning. Balancing of mind (Chapter 10) is a way of living that allows you to enjoy more aspects of your life in a more fulfilling way. It is about making specific choices that give you the opportunity to feel your best for as long as you can.

The mind operates as a powerful tool for creating your experiences. Every invention, from the wheel to space voyage, was born from human thought and imagination. The chapter Power of Mind delves into the mind's potential to influence thoughts, emotions and actions. The human mind is an intricate and power entity, holding vast untapped potential within its depths. It's often said that only a small fraction of your mental capacity is used in daily life.

The chapter Ultimate Use of Mind highlights how to maximize the mind's potential for personal growth and transformation. The mind is limitless, capable of soaring beyond physical boundaries, exploring the furthest reaches of imagination or understanding the deepest layers of reality. It emphasizes cultivating clarity, focus, and critical thinking while balancing logic.

The chapter Mind: A Tool for Divinity explores the mind as a bridge between human and the divine. Beneath the turbulent and tearing thoughts of your mind, there is a state of pure, calm awareness. When you turn your focus inward by curtailing all senses, the mind can stat to taste or experience this blissful consciousness. This is a process that demands constant practice, patience as the mind gradually starts loosening the strings of attachments to temporary things.

The concluding chapter "Beyond Mind" speaks of transcending the mind and not to escape it, but to recognize its nature as a launching-pad rather than the essence of your being. The path beyond the mind begins with observing the subtle spaces of silence and gaps, using them as getaways to the infinite awareness that lies within. It is in this journey that one truly understands the deeper truth that transcends all thoughts.

ॐ पूर्णमदः पूर्णमिदं पूर्णात पूर्णमुदच्यते।

पूर्णस्य पूर्णमादाय पूर्णमेवावशिष्यते॥

ॐ शांतिः शांतिः शांतिः॥

--OM--